999

Structured Pro

Structured Program Design

Using JSP

Rod S. Burgess, MSc., BSc., FBCS
Head of Department of Computing, Newcastle-upon-Tyne Polytechnic

Stanley Thornes (Publishers) Ltd

Originally published 1987 by Hutchinson Education
Reprinted 1988

Reprinted 1990 by
Stanley Thornes (Publishers) Ltd
Old Station Drive
Leckhampton
CHELTENHAM GL53 0DN

British Library Cataloguing in Publication Data

Burgess, Rod, S.
   Structured program design using JSP.—
   2nd ed.
   1. Jackson structured programming
   I. Title   II. Burgess, Rod S. Introduction
   to structured program design using JSP
   005.1′13   QA76.6

ISBN 0 7487 0360 8

Set in 10 on 11½pt Plantin

Printed and bound in Great Britain at
The Bath Press, Avon.

Contents

Editor's note

This book is one of a series of textbooks with a modular structure aimed at students of computer studies and designed for use on courses at most levels of academic and professional qualification. A coherent approach to the development of courses in computing has emerged over the last few years with the introduction of the BTEC National, Higher National and Post-Experience Awards in Computer Studies. The syllabus guidelines for these courses have provided the focus for this series of books, and this ensures that the books are relevant to a wide range of courses at intermediate level.

Many existing books on computing cause frustration to teachers and students because, in trying to be all embracing, they usually include irrelevant material and fail to tackle relevant material in adequate depth. The books in this series are specific in their treatment of topics and practical in their orientation. They provide a firm foundation in all the key areas of computer studies, which are seen as: computer technology; programming the computer; analysing and designing computer-based systems; and applications of the computer.

Currently there are fourteen books in the series. *Computer Appreciation and BASIC Programming* is the introductory book. It is intended to put the computer into context both for the layman who wants to understand a little more about computers and their usage, and for the student as a background for further study.

Computing in a Small Business is aimed specifically at the small businessman, or at the student who will be working in a small business, and sets out to provide a practical guide to implementing computer-based systems in a small business. It is a comprehensive treatment of most aspects of computing.

Fundamentals of Computing looks in considerably more depth than the previous two books at the basic concepts of the technology. Its major emphasis is on hardware, with an introduction to system software. *Computer Systems: Software and architecture* develops from this base and concentrates on software, especially operating systems, language processors and data base management systems; it concludes with a section on networks. *Microprocessors and Industrial Control* aims to provide a fairly complete description and understanding of a general microprocessor-based system with an emphasis on industrial/control applications. Other aspects of computer technology will be addressed by planned books on graphics, real-time embedded systems, and robotics/CIM.

Structured Progam Design is about how to design computer programs based on the Michael Jackson method. Examples of program code are given in BASIC, Pascal and COBOL, but this is not a book about a programming language. A sequel to this book which concentrates on PASCAL programming using JSP is *Jackson Structured Programming with PASCAL*. *Scientific Programming* aims to give a broad and practical view of scientific computing, developing necessary concepts while also revealing some of the problems inherent in solution by computer. Further books are planned in the software area to cover relational databases, systems software and software engineering.

Data Processing Methods provides a fairly detailed treatment of the methods which lie behind computer-based systems in terms of modes of processing, input and output of data, storage of data, and security of systems. Several applications are described. *Information Systems* follows it up by looking at the role of data processing in organizations. This book deals with organizations and their information systems as systems, and with how information systems contribute to and affect the functioning of an organization. Two other books are under development in the area of the application of computers to business; one looks at the business environment for computer-based systems, and the other at the use of decision support and expert systems.

Basic Systems Analysis offers an introduction to the knowledge and skills required by a systems analyst, with rather more emphasis on feasibility, investigation, implementation and review than on design. *Basic Systems Design*, the related volume, tackles design in considerable depth and looks at current methods of structured systems design. *Management of Systems Development* aims to give the reader the skills to plan and monitor systems development projects as well as an understanding of the policy-making and strategic planning required in information systems development. Further titles in the systems analysis and design area are planned to cover human computer interaction issues and automation of system design. *Case Studies in Business Computing* is the final book in the series at the moment, and provides a large number of case studies with questions to provide practical work in most areas of computing work. The exercises are all based on real life, and suggested solutions are available separately to bona fide teachers.

The books in this series stand alone, but all are related to each other so that duplication is avoided.

Barry S. Lee
Series editor

Preface

This book is an enhanced second edition of *Introduction to Program Design using JSP* by the same author.

The book is about how to design programs, in particular for data processing applications. There are now a number of well-established program design techniques, and the one chosen for this text is that of Michael Jackson, called Jackson Structured Programming (JSP). It is the most common of the formalized techniques used in Europe, particularly in the UK. Its use in education within the UK is also widespread; it is used by many institutions of higher education as the main design method taught to students following BTEC Higher National courses in computer studies and degree courses in computing with a commercial data processing orientation.

This enhanced text covers all aspects of the JSP design method, including a detailed treatment of the more difficult techniques of inversion and backtracking which were not included in the original book.

The book has also been enhanced as regards first, coverage of interactive and network database program design, and second, the use of the flowschema in the testing of JSP-designed programs.

The book assumes that the reader has already some knowledge of computers and data processing systems as well as some experience of elementary programming, such as would be derived from a course of study based upon two other books in this series, namely *Computer Appreciation and Basic Programming* by Allan McHattie and Jennifer Ward and *Data Processing Methods* by Barry Lee. In particular, the reader should have an understanding of subroutines and parameter passing before attempting Chapter 8

and an understanding of Codasyl network databases (e.g. IDMS) before attempting Chapter 11.

The text is intended for use in conjunction with first, a text on the specific programming language being used, preferably one that relates in some way to JSP, and second, a text that looks at all aspects of the programming task.

Heavy use is made of examples throughout the text, and in addition the majority of chapters conclude with exercises for the reader; solutions to the exercises are presented at the end of the book. Where there is a need to illustrate with programming language code, examples are given in COBOL, BASIC and Pascal. However, this book is *not* about a programming language but about a program design method which is programming-language independent.

The book is not intended to be a reference text but one in which the chapters need to be read in sequential order. Programming, in particular program design, is essentially a practical skill that can only be obtained by practice and experience. Hence the exercises at the end of each chapter are not intended to be optional for the reader, but are a necessary part of the activity of reading the text. The author has assumed, in writing each chapter, that the exercises of the previous chapter have been attempted by the reader, with a reasonable degree of success.

Even though the JSP design method is intended to be language independent, it cannot be divorced entirely from the other tasks associated with the programming activity. Hence although the major part of the text concentrates on the design technique itself, Chapters 7, 10 and 12 examine the impact of using JSP on the associated programming tasks of coding, testing and optimization respectively.

Acknowledgements

The first acknowledgement must be of course to
M. A. Jackson, whose book *Principles of Program
Design* introduced me to his technique and
enabled me for the first time to really teach my
students how to design programs in a non-
intuitive way.

The other acknowledgement goes to the
multitude of colleagues and students who have
shared with me the experience of teaching,
learning and practising JSP.

1 Introduction

The primary aim of this book is to explain and demonstrate a particular design method which is used internationally by data processing professionals.

It is an assumption of this book that you have been introduced to some of the skills of programming by writing a few elementary programs. In most of your cases these programs will have been written to solve problems set by your tutors. It is another assumption of this book that you intend to continue to learn more about programming and write more programs with a view to entering the data processing profession as a programmer. It is, therefore, important at an early stage in your programming education that you obtain some appreciation of the programming task as practised by the professionals and of the qualities expected of their programs. Only then perhaps will you appreciate the content of this book and realize its importance to your endeavour to improve the quality of your programming and programs, so that you may be better prepared to go out and meet the needs and challenges of the programming profession.

Some important characteristics of real programs

As a starting-point it is beneficial to identify some of the major differences between the problems and programs with which you have been involved up to now ('novice' programs) and those you will be involved with as a professional programmer ('real' programs).

Novice problems and programs have the following significant characteristics:

The problems are relatively small and simple, characterized by the ease with which they may be specified in a few sentences on a sheet of paper and comprehended in minutes. They are intentionally small and simple because the aim is for you to quickly get some practice in the use of a programming language and a computer, and to build up your confidence in their use.

The major difficulties that you have experienced in writing these programs, therefore, have not been with understanding the problems to be solved or the way to solve them. Indeed, students often say that the problems and their solutions are so easy that it is quicker to solve them by hand than write a program to solve them. The difficulties have been with expressing the solutions in programming language terms and demonstrating that the programs work on the computer.

The program development time is relatively short.
The time taken for you to write a program to solve a given problem and demonstrate that it works, i.e. the development time, can be measured in hours. Consequently it has not been difficult for you to mentally hold and maintain details of all aspects of the program throughout the period of its development. Furthermore it is likely that you will have tested your program with, at the most, a few random test cases.

The life of the programs is relatively short. When you have completed a program and demonstrated to your tutor that it works, the life of the program is usually terminated. The only other person who is likely to read and review your programs is your tutor.

The programs were not intended for use. The programs you have written were not intended to be used by other people, in particular non-programmers, as a tool or as part of their day-to-day work.

Real problems and their programs, by contrast, have the following characteristics:

The problems are relatively large and/or complex. Typical data processing programs are written for problems for which, because of their size and/or complexity, it is difficult to mentally hold and maintain details. To aid comprehension of these problems it is necessary to specify them more formally on a number of sheets of paper. Comprehension time is usually measured in hours or days rather than minutes. The major difficulties that are experienced in writing these programs are with understanding the problem, ensuring that the programmer's understanding of the problem agrees with the person who specified the problem (usually the systems analyst), and designing a solution to the problem suitable for conversion into a programming language.

The development time is relatively long. Development times of data processing programs are measured in weeks or months. Consequently it is difficult for the programmer to retain and remember all aspects of the program throughout its development. He therefore needs to continuously document everything he does in a systematic way throughout the development period, so that he may more easily recall information about actions taken earlier.

The life of the programs is relatively long. A typical data processing program remains in use for a time measured in years. During this time a particular program may be executed hundreds or thousands of times, with perhaps billions of different combinations of data, consuming perhaps thousands of hours of computer elapsed time. Furthermore, during its life it may undergo many changes because, for instance, it needs to be transferred to another computer system or it needs to solve a slightly changed problem. The majority of these changes are likely to be carried out by programmers other than the one who wrote the program. A professional programmer must ensure that he minimizes the risk of his program 'crashing' during its production life and that he minimizes the effort required to change his program, whatever the reason.

Programs are written for use by other people. A data processing program, like any other product, is made for use by people. Like any other product, e.g. a TV set, to be good it must meet certain quality criteria; for instance, it must be easy to use, it shouldn't malfunction very often, and if it does malfunction then it should be possible to put it right as quickly as possible.

The significant conclusions arising out of this comparison of 'novice' and 'real' problems and programs are:

1   Real programs take a considerable time to develop and are in use for an even longer time.
2   There are other quality criteria, besides the one that the program should work, by which the 'goodness' of a program is judged.
3   In handling real programs the major difficulties are not usually in using the programming language but with, for instance, understanding the problem to be solved and designing a solution suitable for translation into a programming language.

In the remainder of this chapter the notion of the 'program life cycle' will be introduced, together with a brief discussion of the quality criteria that might be used to judge 'the goodness of a program'. This will lead to a discussion on the need for good program design as a means of making the activities within the program life cycle more effective and efficient and ensuring the increased goodness of a program.

The program life cycle

It is possible to identify a number of distinct stages in the life of a program:

Specification
There must be a detailed specification of the problem, i.e. what the programmer is required to do. It will usually be in written form and will specify the inputs and outputs to the program and what processing the program will need to do in order to transform the inputs into outputs. It may contain other information such as computer requirements. The specification is usually not

produced by the programmer himself but rather by a systems analyst or senior programmer.

Design
A design must be derived from an analysis of the requirements of the program contained in the program specification. The design is usually expressed in some diagrammatic form and the level of detail is such that the translation into program language statements is straightforward.

Implementation
The program design must be converted into the programming language and executed on the computer.

Testing
The implemented program must be tested with suitable data to ensure that it meets the requirements of the original program specification.

Operation and maintenance
The program must be installed and used. When errors are discovered these must be corrected. Changes to the program may be required because of changes to the original requirements of the program.

The first four stages of this cycle are commonly referred to as 'program development'.

Although the program life cycle outlined above has been described as a sequence of distinct stages, that is not to say that each of these stages is self-contained or that the process of program development is wholly sequential. Indeed the process is partially iterative with each stage in the life cycle feeding back information to earlier stages. As programming proceeds, details of the specification may be clarified or even changed, leading to changes in stages thought to be complete. Implementation may show up errors in design. Testing may show up errors in coding or design. When the program is in operation errors not previously identified will be discovered. As a result of using the program, users may identify changes in their requirements leading to changes in the program. As a result of these events parts of earlier stages in the cycle may have to be repeated.

Another important characteristic of the program life cycle is that each stage accounts for an unequal proportion of the programmer's time and, therefore, of the total costs of the program. Surveys that have been carried out in typical data processing departments indicate that programmer time associated with maintenance far exceeds that associated with the initial program development; factors of two or more are not untypical. Within the program development stages these surveys indicate that typically 40 per cent of programmer time is spent on program specification analysis and program design, 20 per cent on implementation and 40 per cent on testing.

Qualities of a good program

When you go out to select and purchase a product, say a car, then if you are going to do the selection properly you will prepare and take with you a ranked list of criteria against which you will assess the 'goodness' of each car that you see. These criteria might include, for a car, maximum price, number of doors, colour, engine size etc. If a friend also goes out to purchase a car he may have a similar list of critera. The two lists will undoubtedly have common criteria; however, he may have some not on your list and vice versa, and furthermore his ranking of the common criteria may be different from yours. The conclusion from this analogy is that if a number of people assess a number of similar products, although the majority of criteria used may be common, undoubtedly the rankings of criteria in order of importance will be different.

Similarly it is possible to identify the commonest qualities used, by the data processing profession at large, to assess the goodness of a program. However, the ranking of these qualities in order of importance and the stress placed on each quality may vary from one data processing department to another, and even from one program to another in the same data processing department.

What are the commonest quality criteria used to assess the goodness of programs?

Correctness, i.e. the program does what it is supposed to do.
Usability, i.e. the program is easy to use by the people for whom it is written.
Maintainability, i.e. if any amendments are required to the program they are easily carried out.
Efficiency, i.e. the program uses the computer resources efficiently.

There can be no doubt that correctness is the primary quality of any program. The program must process correctly all data, including exceptional data, presented to it throughout its operational life. However, this is not the only criterion by which the majority of programs are judged to be good.

Another important criterion is their usability; this is particularly important for programs which interact directly with their users at terminals, for instance.

In the previous section of this chapter it was identified that the maintenance of a program can occupy a very significant amount of programmer time, and therefore the ease with which amendments can be made to a program must also be a major quality of a program, particularly one that has a long operational life.

In the early days of computers and programming the efficiency of a program was usually very high in anybody's list of criteria for a good program. Those were the days of relatively limited and expensive primary storage, slow CPU processing time and slow peripherals. Times have changed and we now have relatively cheap and fast computer systems, and therefore the efficiency criterion usually takes a low priority.

The importance of program design

This book is primarily about program design, the stage within the program life cycle that has been identified by the data processing profession as having the most significant impact on the other stages of the life cycle and on the degree of goodness of the resulting program.

Program maintenance has been identified as the most programmer time-consuming stage in the program life cycle. Also, if you ask any experienced programmer which aspect of programming he dislikes most, then 99 times out of 100 he will identify program maintenance. Why is this so? Perhaps there are two major reasons. First, because most programmers enjoy the creative aspects of program development, i.e. creating something from nothing! Second, because most programs written by other people are difficult to understand, and understandability is a prime requirement for speedy and effective maintenance. The message therefore is that, if the programmer is to spend less time on maintenance and more time on the more creative task of program development, programmers will have to learn to write programs which are more understandable and more easily modified.

Another major stage in the program life cycle is that of testing, both because it consumes a significant amount of programmer time and because it is the time when the programmer demonstrates the correctness of his program. The programmer must therefore look for ways by which he can maximize the correctness of his program in the shortest possible time. First, he must look for ways by which he can minimize the number of errors he puts into his program in the stages prior to testing; remember that many errors occur in a program because programmers put them there! Second, he should be able to identify, as easily as possible, the tests required to thoroughly test his program. Third, the location and correction of errors in the program should be achievable quickly and effectively.

It is during these two major stages, i.e. testing and maintenance, that program design can have the greatest impact. A good program design method can lead to sound programs that are more easily understood and modified by somebody else and that are easier to test thoroughly. The rest of this book is about a particular program design method, called Jackson Structured Programming (JSP), which has shown itself in practice to lead to these qualities in a program because it has the following characteristics:

It is a closely knit and formalized method. It is less intuitive, less subject to trial and error, and less dependent on experience than other program design methods. It is also teachable and can be learnt – hence this book.

It tends to produce standard results, i.e. the same problem given to a number of JSP programmers will lead to very similar programs. This helps programmers maintain others' programs. It also enables greater management and quality control of programmers' work, and hence increases the likelihood of more correct programs.

Documentation is an integral part of the method, and hence it is more likely that accurate and complete documentation will be produced; that is a necessity for efficient and effective maintenance.

The structure of the program design is modelled on the structure of the problem. This means that the programmer is encouraged to obtain a good understanding of the problem, i.e. program specification, before design starts. The majority of program errors have been demonstrated to arise from errors in the program specification and the programmer's incomplete or inaccurate understanding of the program specification. Hence the method is likely to lead to more correct programs. Also the majority of maintenance work arises out of changes to the problem; hence using JSP should make it easier to translate changes in the problem to changes in the design.

It enables the easier identification of test data, and hence is likely to lead to more thorough testing.

Exercises

1.1 Talk to an experienced practising programmer and discuss with him the issues raised in this chapter.

1.2 Take a friend's finished program and attempt to understand it and modify it to meet slightly changed requirements agreed between you and him. Choose a reasonably large program of say 50 statements or more.

2 The fundamentals of Jackson Structured Program design

You have a better chance of designing programs that meet the goodness criteria of correctness and maintainability if a systematic approach to program design is adopted. There are a number of well-known and well-used systematic methods of program design; in particular, over the last decade a number of so-called 'structured design' methods have become popular. One of these structured design methods, JSP, is especially popular in Europe. This method has shown itself to be very successful at producing very reliable and maintainable data processing programs. The rest of this book is concerned with presenting to you the basics of the method. Two books already exist on JSP, namely Michael Jackson's book *Principles of Program Design*[1] and Leif Ingevaldsson's book *JSP – A Practical Method of Program Design*[2]. JSP was in fact designed by Michael Jackson.

Jackson based his program design method on two fundamental principles of structured program design identified by other programming pioneers, namely the process of 'stepwise refinement' and the principle that all programs can be designed using only three 'structured control constructs'. Jackson added a third principle of 'data structure-based design'.

The first section of this chapter presents a sample program designed using JSP and written in a program description language rather than a particular programming language. This program is used throughout the chapter for illustrative purposes. The second, third and fourth sections explain the three fundamental principles of JSP, namely:

1 Stepwise refinement
2 The use of the three structured control constructs
3 Data structure-based design.

The third section also introduces the JSP structure diagram used for documenting a JSP design. The fifth section of the chapter presents an overview of the JSP design method.

The sample program and the program description language

The sample program to be used for illustrative purposes in this chapter is written to meet the requirements of the following program specification:

Example 2.1 *Demerge program*
An input sequential file contains two types of records, the type of record being identified by the character 1 or 2 in the first character position of the record. The input file is terminated by an end-of-file record.

A program is required to input the records from this file and output all type 1 records to one output file and all type 2 records to a second output file. Both output files should be in the same key sequence as the input file and each should be terminated by an end-of-file record. Any records not of type 1 or 2 should be output to a report but otherwise ignored. The report will be terminated by an end-of-report message.

The overall requirement of this program could be summarized as to demerge (i.e. the opposite to merge) the input file into two output files.

The program for this specification is given in Figure 2.1. The program is presented using not a particular programming language, which might confuse readers unfamiliar with that particular language, but rather an informal language having characteristics similar to many high-level programming languages.

The informal language used to describe the sample program will be referred to in the remainder of this book as 'the program description language'. As this language will be used for describing other programs in this book, some explanation of it is required.

The 'words' in italics are the only formal parts

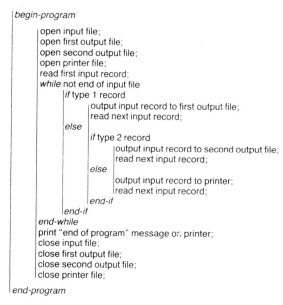

```
begin-program
    open input file;
    open first output file;
    open second output file;
    open printer file;
    read first input record;
    while not end of input file
        if type 1 record
            output input record to first output file;
            read next input record;
        else
            if type 2 record
                output input record to second output file;
                read next input record;
            else
                output input record to printer;
                read next input record;
            end-if
        end-if
    end-while
    print "end of program" message on printer;
    close input file;
    close first output file;
    close second output file;
    close printer file;
end-program
```

Figure 2.1   *Demerge program*

of the language and, if you like, the 'reserved' words of the language.

The delimiters of a program, i.e. its beginning and end, are indicated by the reserved words *begin-program* and *end-program*. The main body of the program consists of 'actions' and 'control constructs'.

Actions are equivalent to imperative statements in high-level programming languages and usually have a one-to-one, or at the most one-to-few, relationship with programming language statements. Actions are specified in 'free expression' English, and each action is terminated by a semicolon. Examples of such actions from the sample program are:

    read first input record;
    output input record to second output file;
    print 'end of program' message on printer;

The control constructs are equivalent to conditional control statements in a high-level programming language. There are two types of control construct in the program description language, namely iteration (*while* construct) and selection (*if . . . else* construct).

Iterations indicate a repetitious situation (i.e. 'while a condition is true keep repeating a specified component (i.e. part) of the program'). The sample program contains an example of an iteration construct, namely:

while not end of input file

} program component which is repeated

end-while

The limits of the program component to be repeated are indicated by the reserved words *while* and *end-while*. The program component contained within an iteration construct may consist of one or more actions and/or further control constructs – indeed, possible further iteration constructs. The condition that dictates if the program component is to be repeated follows the *while* word and is specified in free expression English.

Selections indicate that the next component of the program to be executed will be chosen from one of two different program components depending on whether a condition is true or false. An example of a selection can be taken from the sample program, namely:

if type 1 record

} program component A

else

} program component B

end-if

The limits of the selection construct are indicated by *if* and *end-if* reserved words. The condition that dictates which of the two program components is to be executed follows the *if* and is specified in free expression English. The program component to be executed if the condition is 'true' is delimited by the *if* and *else* words, and the program component to be executed if the condition is 'false' is delimited by the *else* and *end-if* words. The two program components contained within a selection construct may consist of one or more actions and/or further control constructs – indeed, possibly further selection constructs. An example of the latter is contained within the sample program, where program component B consists of another selection construct:

if type 2 record

$\left.\begin{array}{c} \\ \\ \end{array}\right\}$ program component B1

else

$\left.\begin{array}{c} \\ \\ \end{array}\right\}$ program component B2

end-if

The combination of two or more selection constructs in this way is often referred to as 'multiway' selection.

The last characteristic of the language that needs explaining is the use of the indentation (highlighted by vertical lines indicating margins), which is used for readability to emphasize the limits of the program components contained between the *begin-program . . . end-program, if . . . else . . . end-if*, and *while . . . end-while* delimiter words.

The two fundamental principles of structured program design

All structured program design methods, including JSP, are based upon the two fundamental principles of 'stepwise refinement' and 'three structured control constructs'. These two principles will now be explained.

The objective of program design, whichever design method is used, is to transform the required function of the program, as stated in the program specification, into a set of instructions which can be easily translated into a chosen programming language. This transformation can be achieved in one step for very simple programs, but for more complex programs a different approach must be adopted. The process of stepwise refinement is such an approach: in it the stated program function is broken down (i.e. refined) into subsidiary functions in progressively increasing levels of detail until the lowest-level functions are achievable in the programming language. The process can be crudely likened to the process of smashing a very large rock into very small pieces. It would take a superman, or a very brittle rock, to achieve this objective in one swing of a sledgehammer. The only effective and efficient approach that could be adopted would be

to smash the rock into progressively smaller and smaller pieces of rock.

The second fundamental principle of structured program design is that any program can be constructed using only three structured control constructs. A control construct is a program component which can only be entered from the beginning of the component and can only be exited from the end of the component, i.e. a 'one entry and one exit' component. In structured program design there are only three types of control constructs allowed, namely sequences, iterations and selections. The last two may be equated with the corresponding control constructs in the program description language described in the previous section. The sample program can be used to illustrate these three constructs.

Sequence
A sequence is a program component which has two or more parts (subcomponents) occurring once each, in order. The whole sample program can be viewed as a sequence of three subcomponents as shown in Figure 2.2.

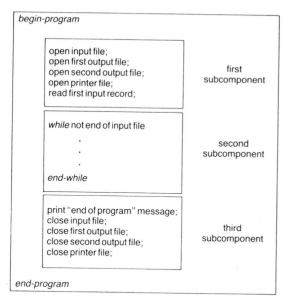

Figure 2.2   *Sequence component*

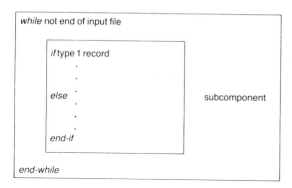

Figure 2.3   *Iteration component*

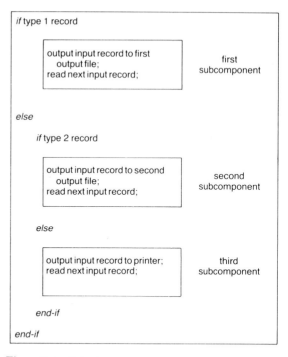

Figure 2.4   *Selection component*

Iteration

An iteration is a program component which has only one part, occurring zero or more times. The second subcomponent in Figure 2.2 is an example of an iteration of one subcomponent as illustrated in Figure 2.3. The number of times the subcomponent will be executed depends upon when the condition 'not end of input file' becomes false, i.e. when the end of input file is reached. This may occur on first entry to the iteration component, i.e. when the first record input is the end-of-file record, or after a number of repetitions of the subcomponent.

Selection

A selection is a program component that has two or more parts, of which one, and only one, occurs once. The subcomponent identified in Figure 2.3 is an example of a selection of three subcomponents, as illustrated in Figure 2.4. The subcomponent executed will depend on the record type of the input record being processed:

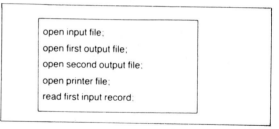

Figure 2.5   *Elementary component*

Original requirement

```
DEMERGE FILE PROGRAM
```

First refinement

```
begin-program
    PROGRAM INITIALIZATION
    PROGRAM BODY
    PROGRAM TERMINATION
end-program
```

Second refinement

```
begin-program

    open input file;
    open first output file;
    open second output file;
    open printer file;
    read first input record;

    while not end of input file
        PROCESS RECORD
    end-while

    print "end of program" message;
    close input file;
    close first output file;
    close second output file;
    close printer file;

end-program
```

Third refinement

```
begin-program
    open input file;
    open first output file;
    open second output file;
    open printer file;
    read first input record;
    while not end of input file

        if type 1 record
            PROCESS TYPE 1 RECORD
        else
            if type 2 record
                PROCESS TYPE 2 RECORD
            else
                PROCESS INVALID RECORD
            end-if

    end-while

    print "end of program" message;
    close input file;
    close first output file;
    close second output file;
    close printer file;

end-program
```

Figure 2.6   *Application of the two fundamental structured design principles (see text on page 24)*

Fourth and final refinement

```
begin-program

    open input file;
    open first output file;
    open second output file;
    open printer file;
    read first input record;
    while not end of input file

        if type 1 record
            output input record to first output file;
            read next input record;
        else
            if type 2 record
                output input record to second output file;
                read next input record;
            else
                output input record to printer;
                read next input record;
        end-if

    end-while

    print "end of program" message;
    close input file;
    close first output file;
    close second output file;
    close printer file;

end-progam
```

If record type is 1, then the first subcomponent will be executed.
If record type is 2, then the second subcomponent will be executed.
If record type is neither 1 nor 2, then the third subcomponent will be executed.

For completeness it ought to be mentioned at this stage that there is a fourth type of component, the elementary component, which is not a control component but which is required, together with the three control components, to construct any program. An elementary component has no subcomponents but consists of a sequence of one or more imperative actions as illustrated in Figure 2.5.

Having explained the two fundamental principles of structured program design separately, we can now bring them together to produce a definition of structured program design. The process of structured program design is an approach whereby the stated program function is broken down into subsidiary functions in progressively increasing levels of detail until the lowest-level functions are achievable in the programming language. At each step of the refinement a function is broken down only as a sequence of subfunctions, an iteration of a subfunction or a selection of two or more subfunctions.

The sample program in Figure 2.1 was produced using the structured program design method JSP, but it could have been produced just using the two fundamental principles of structured program design. The process is illustrated in Figure 2.6, where the result of each stage of the refinement process is shown by representing the newly refined subfunctions as full-line boxes and the functions from which they were refined as dotted-line boxes. Those functions achievable in the programming language are represented in lower case, and those functions that require further refining, i.e. components, are represented in upper case.

JSP hierarchical structure diagrams

The progress of the structured program design process as illustrated in Figure 2.6 is often represented in diagrammatic form using some form of 'hierarchical structure diagram'. An example of such a hierarchical structure diagram, the type used in JSP, is given in Figure 2.7 and relates to the design process illustrated in Figure 2.6.

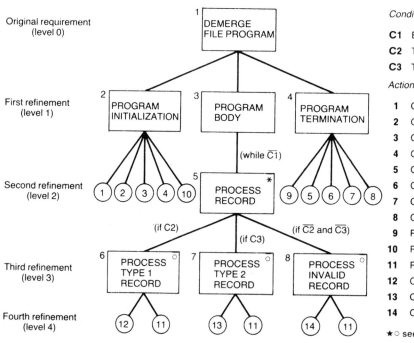

Figure 2.7   *A JSP program structure diagram*

Each level of the structure diagram represents a refinement of the level immediately above it. The levels, starting with the highest (i.e. the total program function), are usually referred to by the numbers 0, 1, 2 etc. corresponding to the stages in the refinement process illustrated in Figure 2.6. Each box represents a function of the program, which is further refined at the next level down either into a sequence, iteration or selection of subsidiary functions, or into an elementary component of detailed actions achievable in the target programming language.

Hence the refinement of a function A into a sequence of three subfunctions B, C and D is represented in a JSP structure diagram as shown in Figure 2.8.

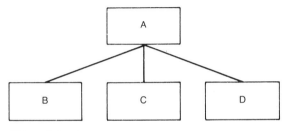

Figure 2.8   *A sequence program component*

The refinement of a function F as an iteration of subfunction G while condition C is true is represented in a JSP structure diagram as shown in Figure 2.9. Note the use of the asterisk (*) in

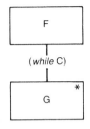

Figure 2.9   *An iteration program component*

the top right-hand corner of the box representing the function being iterated.

The refinement of a function H as a selection of three subfunctions X, Y and Z depending on whether, respectively, conditions C1 or C2 or (neither C1 nor C2) is true, is represented in a JSP structure diagram as shown in Figure 2.10. Note the use of the circle (°) in the top right-hand corner of the boxes representing the functions being selected.

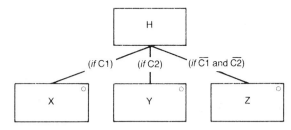

Figure 2.10   *A selection program component*

Conditions associated with iterations and selections are listed separately from the structure diagram and cross-referenced to the structure diagram using condition numbers C1, C2 etc. The negative of a condition is represented by a bar over the condition number.

The refinement of a function S as a sequence of actions (1 followed by 2 followed by 3) achievable in the target programming language, i.e. S is an elementary function, is represented in a JSP structure diagram as shown in Figure 2.11.

Figure 2.11   *An elementary program component*

Note that actions are also listed separately from the structure diagram and cross-referenced to the structure diagram by using the action numbers contained in 'bubbles' linked to the elementary component(s) to which they refer.

The third fundamental principle of JSP

JSP is a structured program design method and therefore employs the two fundamental principles of stepwise refinement and the three structured control constructs. However, what makes JSP distinctive is the principle of basing the program design on the characteristics of the data to be processed by the program.

Data processing programs are concerned with processing data (a fairly obvious thing to say), that is they are concerned with processing data from one or more input files to produce data to be output to one or more output files. Jackson's contention is, therefore, that the processing and hence program design should be dictated by the characteristics of the data being processed. The sample program in Figure 2.1 was derived using the JSP design method, and if we examine the structure of this program we can indeed see the characteristics of the data, in particular the input data file, reflected in the design.

The first characteristic of the input data file is that it contains a number of data records terminated by an end-of-file record. Each of these records must be processed by the program, and we can see this characteristic reflected in the program in the iteration where the program component being iterated will process one record ánd will be repeated for each record until the end-of-file record is input:

while not end of input file

| PROCESS RECORD |

end-while

The second characteristic of the input data file is that each record may be either of type 1 or of type 2 or invalid. This characteristic of the data is reflected in the selection where, in processing one input record, one of three program components will be executed depending on whether the input record is of type 1 or type 2 or invalid:

if type 1 record

| PROCESS TYPE 1 RECORD |

else

    if type 2 record

    | PROCESS TYPE 2 RECORD |

    else

    | PROCESS INVALID RECORD |

    end-if
end-if

Having hopefully convinced you that there is some substance to the contention that a workable program design can reflect the characteristics of the data being processed by the program, we now need to discuss how Jackson has incorporated this idea into his design method.

What follows is a brief overview of the JSP design method.

Overview of the JSP design method

The JSP design method consists of a number of steps, depicted in Figure 2.12. These steps will now be described in outline, using the sample program as a vehicle, leaving a more detailed description of each step to later chapters of this book.

Step 1   Produce data structures
The starting point of JSP is to analyse the characteristics of each input and output data file to be processed by the program, as described in the program specification, using the two fundamental principles of structured program

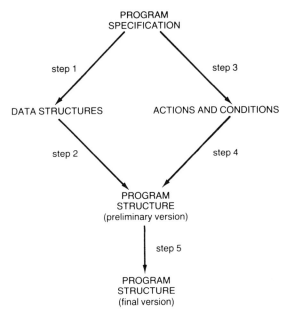

Figure 2.12 *JSP steps*

design. The results of this analysis are represented as a hierarchical structure diagram (a data structure diagram). For Example 2.1 four such data structure diagrams would be produced, one for the input file and one for each of the three output files. For example, the data structure diagram for the input file would be as depicted in Figure 2.13.

If the data structure diagram in Figure 2.13 is compared with the eventual program structure diagram in Figure 2.7, a close relationship can be identified.

Step 2   Produce preliminary version of program structure

The next step is to combine the data structures produced in the first step to produce the preliminary version of the program structure. In the case of the example this would result in a program structure (see Figure 2.14, overleaf) whose skeleton coincides with that of the input file data structure depicted in Figure 2.13.

Step 3   Identify actions and conditions

The program specification is again examined and the detailed processing necessary to produce the output data from the input data is considered. From this analysis a list of all conditions and actions (achievable in the programming language) is extracted. In the case of Example 2.1 the list would be as given in Figure 2.15 (overleaf).

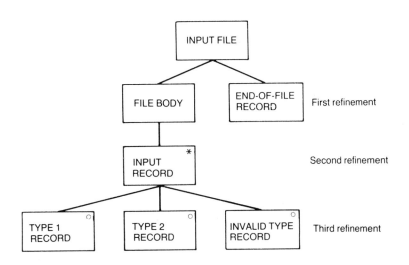

Figure 2.13 *Data structure diagram*

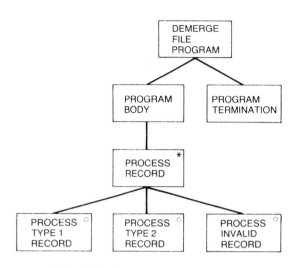

Figure 2.14   *Preliminary program structure*

Step 4   Allocate actions and conditions to program structure

Each of the conditions identified in step 3 are taken and allocated, using the condition numbers specified in Figure 2.15, to one or more of the iterations and selections in the program structure diagram derived in step 2. Similarly, each of the actions identified in step 3 is allocated to one or more components in the program structure diagram. The result of this allocation for the example is depicted in Figure 2.16 where the allocated actions are shown using within 'bubbles' the numbers specified in Figure 2.15.

Step 5   Produce final version of program structure

As a result of allocating the actions to the program structure during step 4, the program structure may be invalidated. What this means is that the program structure may not now consist of only sequence, iteration, selection and elementary

Conditions

C1   End of input file?

C2   Type 1 record?

C3   Type 2 record?

Actions

1   Open input file

2   Open first output file

3   Open second output file

4   Open printer file

5   Close input file

6   Close first output file

7   Close second output file

8   Close printer file

9   Print "end of program" message on printer

10   Read first input record

11   Read next input record

12   Output input record to first output file

13   Output input record to second output file

14   Output input record to printer

Figure 2.15   *Condition and action lists*

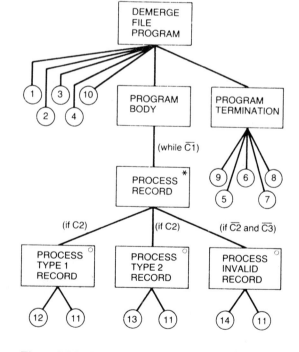

Figure 2.16   *Program structure with allocated actions and conditions*

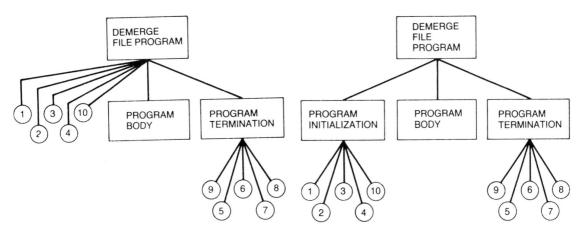

Figure 2.17   *Invalid DEMERGE FILE PROGRAM component*

Figure 2.18   *Revised and valid DEMERGE FILE PROGRAM component*

components. Such a situation has arisen in Figure 2.16, where the component DEMERGE FILE PROGRAM is a mixture of a sequence and an elementary component as highlighted in Figure 2.17.

This invalidity may be overcome by revising the program structure; that is, by adding to the sequence component DEMERGE FILE PROGRAM a further component PROGRAM INITIALIZATION, preceding PROGRAM BODY and PROGRAM TERMINATION, as shown in Figure 2.18.

The resulting program structure is the final version of the program structure, and represents the detailed program design depicted in Figure 2.7.

The detailed program design derived from step 5 can then be converted directly into programming language statements. Alternatively it can first be converted into some intermediate program description language, such as the one described in Example 2.1 or Jackson's Schematic Logic (described in Chapter 7), which can then be converted into the statements of a programming language.

The rest of this book examines in detail the steps outlined in this section.

Exercises

2.1   A validated stores movements file contains two types of record, issue and receipt. An issue record contains the following items: part number, record type (I, indicating an issue record) and quantity issued. A receipt record contains the following items: part number, record type (R, indicating a receipt record) and quantity received. The file is sorted into part number sequence and terminated by an end-of-file record. There may be more than one movement record for a part number.

An analysis of the stores movements file is to be produced as a report on a printer. The report is to contain report headings followed by a one-line report for each part, containing the part number and the total net movement for the part, and ending with a summary line containing the total number of issue records and the total number of receipt records. The analysis report flows heedlessly over any perforations in the printer paper.

A JSP designed program to carry out this function, written in the program description language, is given in Figure 2.19. You may find the line numbers down the left-hand side of the program useful, for reference purposes, in producing your solution to this exercise. You are required to:

(a) Identify the two sequence components, the two iteration components, the selection component and the six elementary components in this program.
(b) List all the actions in the program.
(c) List all the simple conditions in the program.
(d) Identify the parts of the program which directly relate to the following characteristics of the stores movements file and the movements analysis report:
Stores movements file:
The body of the file consists of groups of records for each part;
Each group of records for a part consists of one or more part movement records;
A part movement record may either be an issue record or a receipt record;
Movements analysis report:
The report consists of report headings followed by a report body

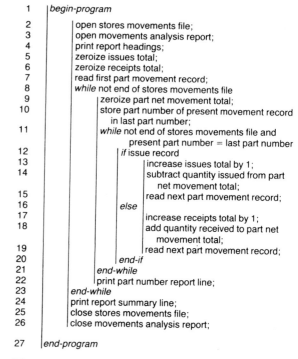

```
1   begin-program
2       open stores movements file;
3       open movements analysis report;
4       print report headings;
5       zeroize issues total;
6       zeroize receipts total;
7       read first part movement record;
8       while not end of stores movements file
9           zeroize part net movement total;
10          store part number of present movement record
                in last part number;
11          while not end of stores movements file and
                    present part number = last part number
12              if issue record
13                  increase issues total by 1;
14                  subtract quantity issued from part
                        net movement total;
15                  read next part movement record;
16              else
17                  increase receipts total by 1;
18                  add quantity received to part net
                        movement total;
19                  read next part movement record;
20              end-if
21          end-while
22          print part number report line;
23      end-while
24      print report summary line;
25      close stores movements file;
26      close movements analysis report;
27  end-program
```

Figure 2.19 *Stores movement program*

(containing part number reports) followed by a summary line; the report body consists of a repetition of part number reports.

(e) Produce the JSP program structure diagram for this program.

3 Producing data structures

The first step in the JSP design method is to analyse the data to be input to, used by and output from the program and to describe its structure using structure diagrams. This chapter is concerned with explaining this process.

For most programs the data that dictates the program design is high-volume data input from, stored on or output to a peripheral device such as a punched-card reader, magnetic disk unit, printer or VDU. Furthermore the data will usually be organized into one or more files and/or a database. In rarer cases the program design may be influenced by low-volume data consisting of a few data values, perhaps input via a punched card or through a keyboard, or data held internally within primary storage, such as a reference (or look-up) table containing constant values.

Within the JSP method the structure of data, be it a file or internal table, is analysed using the same process of stepwise refinement as described in Chapter 2. This process involves taking the data to be analysed and refining it into subsidiary parts (i.e. data components) in progressively increasing levels of detail until further refinement is no longer significant. The progress of this process is documented using a JSP hierarchical data structure diagram, an example of which was given in Figure 2.13, which details each stage (i.e. level) of the refinement process. In progressing from one level of the data structure to the next the programmer must consider for each data component whether further refinement is significant. If it is, the programmer must decide into what subcomponents the data component is to be refined and how these subcomponents are related both to each other and to their parent data component.

The first section of this chapter will identify the commonest types of data component which you are likely to require in describing the structure of data. The second section will identify the types of relationship which may exist between a data component and its subcomponents, and will describe the JSP diagrammatic method for documenting data structures. The second section will also explain certain terms associated with structure diagrams. The last three sections of this chapter will then describe the process by which a data structure diagram may be produced by analysing the data and the program which processes it.

Data components

This section considers the commonest types of data components, categorized in terms of their level of refinement of data, which might be used in the analysis of the structure of particular data. You should already have been introduced to these types of data component in your previous studies, and hence the following descriptions are intended as a revision.

For the vast majority of programs you will write, the program design will be wholly, or mainly, dictated by the structure of the high-volume data, which will be organized into one or more files and/or a database. This chapter concentrates initially on the design of programs whose high-volume data is organized into files, leaving a consideration of programs that process databases until Chapter 11. It should be noted that when designing modules or subroutines using JSP the input/output parameters are likely to be at a lower level than a file, e.g. record, table or item.

File

The file is therefore the highest level of data component representing a collection of related data which is to be input to, used by or output from a program. The data within a file may relate to a particular entity set or to a particular set of events within an organization, e.g. a personnel file contains data about all employees, an order file contains data about all orders placed by customers over a one-week period. The former type of file is usually referred to as a master file and the latter a transactions (or sometimes a movements) file. Furthermore a file could be classified as an input or an output or a stored file. Input files, usually transactions files, could be contained on, for instance, punched cards or magnetic tape or OCR documents, or input via a VDU. Output files could be output to, for instance, magnetic disk or printer. In the latter case the printed report is classified as an output file, as it is in the programming language COBOL. Stored files, usually master files, are commonly held on magnetic media such as disk or tape.

Record

The record is the next highest level of data component usually associated with data organized into files. A record is a collection of data relating to a particular entity or event, e.g. a personnel record contains data about an employee, an order record contains data about one order for a part. A record is related to a file in that a file is a collection of records. Included within the definition of a record is a line within a printed report or a group of closely associated lines, e.g. page headings on a report page.

Item

The item (or field) is usually the lowest level of data component associated with data organized into files. An item is an attribute of an entity or event, e.g. the name of an employee, the order number within an order. An item is related to a record in that a record is a collection of items. One or more of the items, called record keys, within a record will identify it as relating to a specific entity or event, e.g. the employee number will identify a particular employee's personnel record, the order number within an order record will uniquely identify a particular order for a part.

The file, record and item are the three most common types of data component associated with the description of data organized into files. However, there are further types of data component that may be used in the description of data files.

Record group

The record group is a level of refinement of data between the file and the record. A record group is a group of records closely related in some way for processing purposes. Common examples you will come across are a 'batch' of records within a transaction file prior to validation, records with the same key within a sequenced transaction file used to update a similarly sequenced master file, and a page within a paged report.

Group item

The group item is a level of refinement of data between the record and the item. A group item is a group of items closely related in some way for processing purposes. An example might be the day, month and year items within the date-of-birth group item within a personnel record. Within the COBOL programming language these two types of item are distinguished by referring to the item as an elementary item.

Figure 3.1 summarizes the commonest types of data component associated with data files. They are listed in order of level of refinement from highest to lowest, and for each an example is given extracted from the following file description:

Example 3.1   *Orders file*
A transaction file contains a collection of order records, each order record representing a customer's order for a particular part. The records are held in part number sequence, and

Data component	Example
File	Order file
Record group	All order records with same part number
Record	Order record
Group item	Date of order containing day, month and year items
(Elementary) item	Part number

Figure 3.1   *Common data components used in the description of the structure of a data file*

Sales area code ↓	Sales area name ↓
02	S. London
03	N. London
05	Bedfordshire
07	Buckinghamshire
09	Hertfordshire

Figure 3.2 *Sales area reference table*

therefore for a particular part number there may be zero, one or more order records adjacent to each other. Each order record contains a number of items including part number, date of order and order quantity.

As has already been stated, for the vast majority of programs you will write, the program design will be mainly or wholly dictated by the structure of one or more data files processed by the program. However, in some cases the program design may be affected by the structure of data held internally within primary storage. This data may be organized simply as internal records, group items or elementary items. In certain cases, however, the data may be organized into more complex data structures such as a reference table. An example of such a table might be Figure 3.2.

This reference table might be used for translating a sales area code into its corresponding sales area name. Such a table may be viewed simply as a file, held internally within primary storage, where each entry corresponds to a record and consists of two items, namely sales area code and sales area name. Hence the data components used to describe the structure of an external file may also be used to describe internally stored data, in particular tables.

Similarly the structure of low-volume input or output data, such as a parameter card or a control report output to the operator's console, may be described in terms of the data components already introduced.

Relationships between data components and JSP data structure diagrams

In the previous section the commonest types of data component used in the analysis of the structure of data have been identified. This section now looks at the types of relationship which may exist between a component and its subcomponents.

A data component may be related to its subcomponents in one of three ways – as a *sequence*, an *iteration* or a *selection*. These names are the same as those used to describe the three types of relationship that may exist between a program component and its subcomponents as introduced in Chapter 2. It is no accident that there is an equivalence between the names or indeed (as you will see) between the types of relationship, because one of the fundamental principles of JSP (as identified in Chapter 2) is to base the program structure on the structures of the data processed. Each of these types of relationship between data components will now be described.

Sequence
The sequence describes a data component which is refined into two or more subcomponents, occurring once each only, one after the other. The number of subcomponents is constant whatever instance of data, described by the data component, is being considered. For instance a particular record might be refined into six items occurring once each, one after the other.

Iteration
The iteration describes a data component which is refined into a repetition of a single smaller subcomponent of data. The number of times the

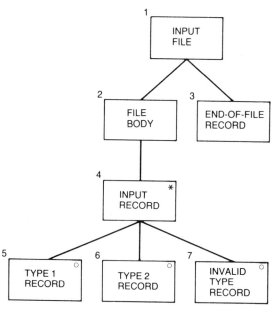

Figure 3.3   *Data structure diagram*

A JSP hierarchical data structure diagram was illustrated in Figure 2.13, and is repeated in Figure 3.3 (box numbers have been added to the diagram for reference purposes).

Within a data structure diagram each component is represented by a rectangular box containing the programmer defined name, always in the singular, for that data component. The topmost box (in Figure 3.3 box 1, INPUT FILE) represents the data whose structure is being described, usually a file or table.

A component which is further refined as a sequence is represented using a notation illustrated by the example in Figure 3.4, extracted from Figure 3.3. Here the INPUT FILE is refined as a *sequence* of the FILE BODY followed by the END-OF-FILE RECORD.

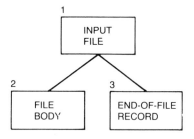

Figure 3.4   *A sequence data component*

subcomponent is repeated may be constant or variable. For instance a look-up table may be refined into a repetition of 20 table entries and a particular file may be refined into a repetition of records, the actual number of records depending on the instance of the file being processed.

Selection
The selection is different in nature from the other two types of relationship. Whereas the sequence and iteration describe components which are refined by breaking them down into smaller subcomponents, the selection describes a component which is not broken down into smaller components but rather consists of one, and one only, of two or more alternative components. For instance, in a transaction file which contains two types of record, a record can be one of two alternative types of record.

Elementary
Not all data components identified in the analysis of the structure of data will be further refined; these components are referred to as elementary components.

A component which is further refined as an iteration is represented using a notation illustrated by the example in Figure 3.5, extracted from Figure 3.3. Here the FILE BODY is refined as an *iteration* of the INPUT RECORD, and is indicated by a single asterisk in the top right-hand corner of the box representing the component INPUT RECORD.

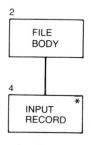

Figure 3.5   *An iteration data component*

A component which is further refined as a selection is represented using a notation illustrated by the example in Figure 3.6, extracted from Figure 3.3. Here the INPUT RECORD is refined as a *selection* of either a TYPE 1 RECORD or a TYPE 2 RECORD or an INVALID TYPE RECORD. This is indicated by a single circle in the top right-hand corner of the boxes representing the components TYPE 1 RECORD, TYPE 2 RECORD and INVALID TYPE RECORD.

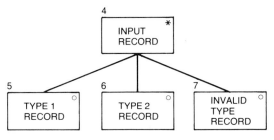

Figure 3.6   *A selection data component*

Components with box numbers 3, 5, 6 and 7 in Figure 3.3 are examples of elementary components, i.e. components that are not further refined. One particular elementary component is the null component, consisting of nothing, which may occur as part of a selection. It is best illustrated by means of an example, as shown in Figure 3.7. This shows that a RECORD GROUP consists of a TYPE 1 RECORD, optionally followed by a TYPE 2 RECORD, followed by a TYPE 3 RECORD.

It is perhaps opportune to explain some more of the terminology associated with structured design and in particular the JSP method. The terminology will be explained with illustrations from the data structure diagram of Figure 3.3, although they apply to structure diagrams in general.

Tree structure. This is an alternative term used to describe the hierarchical structure diagram. If you turn it upside-down perhaps you will get some idea of how the term arose.

Leaves. This term is sometimes used to describe

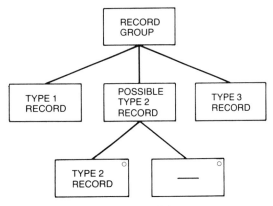

Figure 3.7   *Illustration of a null data component*

the elementary components which are not further refined, i.e. components 3, 5, 6 and 7 in Figure 3.3.

Root. This term is sometimes used to describe the highest-level component, i.e. in Figure 3.3 the INPUT FILE, the data whose structure is being described.

Branch. This term describes that part of a data structure diagram which includes a component and all its descendants (i.e. child components, grandchild components etc.)

Leg. This term describes all those components that lie on the path between the root component and an elementary component. For example 1, 2, 4, 5 represent one leg of the data structure in Figure 3.3.

Level. This term was briefly introduced in Chapter 2; it refers to all the components on the same horizontal level within the structure diagram. For example in Figure 3.3 component 1 is the root component, referred to as level 0, components 2 and 3 on the first level, referred to as level 1, and so on.

Parent and child components. These terms are used in describing the relationship between a component and its subcomponent(s). The former is referred to as the parent (or father) and the latter as the child (or son) component(s). Hence in Figure 3.3 the parent–child relationships are as shown in Figure 3.8.

Parent component	Child component(s)
INPUT FILE	FILE BODY, END-OF-FILE RECORD
FILE BODY	INPUT RECORD
INPUT RECORD	TYPE 1 RECORD, TYPE 2 RECORD, INVALID TYPE RECORD

Figure 3.8   *Parent-child relationships*

Sequenced, selected and iterated components. You have already been introduced to the terms sequence, selection and iteration, which are used to describe the relationship between a parent component and its child component(s) but are specifically used to describe the parent component in the relationship. The terms sequenced, selected and iterated are used to describe the child component(s) in the relationship. Hence, in Figure 3.3, INPUT FILE is a sequence component and FILE BODY and END-OF-FILE RECORD are sequenced components. On the other hand, in the relationship of FILE BODY with INPUT RECORD, FILE BODY is the iteration component and INPUT RECORD is the iterated component. Finally, in the relationship of INPUT RECORD with TYPE 1 RECORD and TYPE 2 RECORD and INVALID TYPE RECORD, INPUT RECORD is the selection component and TYPE 1 RECORD, TYPE 2 RECORD and INVALID TYPE RECORD are the selected components.

Producing a data structure

We have looked at the various concepts associated with analysing the structure of data and the diagrammatic method used to document the progress and result of this analysis. This section will concentrate on the analysis process itself and provide some rules and guidelines on how to produce a correct data structure.

The starting point in the analysis of the structure of data is to identify, from the program specification, each unique data file, internal table etc., for each of which you will need to produce a separate data structure. Concentrating on one of these files etc. you should extract its data description from the program specification; this data description will usually be documented in narrative form and/or in diagrammatic/picture form. Whatever form the data description takes, it will help you to get a clear picture of the data you are analysing if you draw a rough picture of an instance of the data, including all characteristics of the data that you can identify from its description.

Example 3.2   *Unsorted transaction file*
An unsorted transaction file on magnetic tape consists of a set of data records, all of the same type, terminated by an end-of-file record.

A rough picture of this file is shown in Figure 3.9.

Figure 3.9   *A rough picture of unsorted transaction file*

Having produced a clear picture of the data and its characteristics, you are in a position to start analysing the detailed structure using the principles of structured design and representing the structure as a JSP data structure diagram.

Each data component identified during the analysis process is represented by a box containing the data component name, which describes precisely (but concisely, because one of the limitations is the size of the box) the part of the data represented by the component. The majority of the names used in a data structure diagram can be derived from the data description contained in the program specification.

The first component to be identified is always the root component representing the complete data being analysed. In the case of Example 3.2 this is as shown in Figure 3.10.

> UNSORTED
> TRANSACTION
> FILE

Figure 3.10   *Root component for Example 3.2*

The next step is to identify the next level of the data structure, which is to produce a more refined view of the root component. As described earlier in this chapter there are only four ways that a data component may be refined:

1   It may not be refined at all, i.e. it is an elementary component.
2   It may be refined as a sequence of two or more child components, occurring once each, in a definable order. The precise number of child components must also be definable.

3   It may be refined as an iteration of one child component which occurs zero, one or more times. The number of times could be known or depend on the actual instance of the data.
4   It may be refined as a selection of two or more alternative child components where, in a particular instance of the data component, it can only be one of the alternatives. The number of alternatives must be known. It is important with selections to ensure that all possible alternatives are included, especially error situations. The order in which the child components of a selection are documented is not significant.

The rough picture of the data can help identify which refinement alternative applies. In the case of Example 3.2 the UNSORTED TRANSACTION FILE will be refined as a sequence of two subcomponents, occurring once each, in the order FILE BODY (containing the actual data records in the file) and END-OF-FILE RECORD. This refinement is identified within the picture of the file and represented in a JSP data structure diagram as in Figure 3.11.

There are a number of comments to make about this refinement. First, the reader may think that an alternative solution to the first refinement

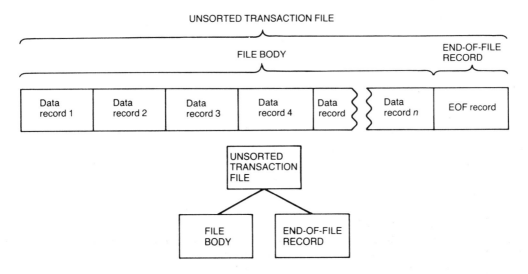

Figure 3.11   *First refinement for Example 3.2*

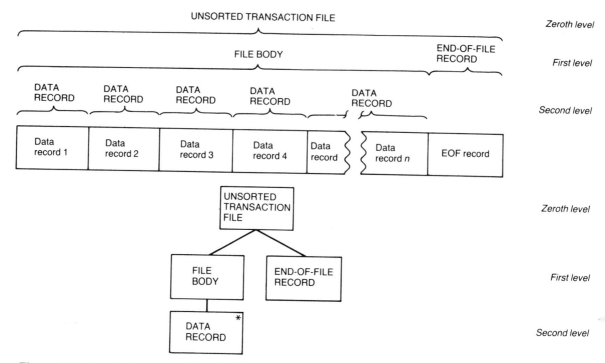

Figure 3.12   *Second refinement for Example 3.2*

was an iteration of 'record'. This solution would in fact be wrong, but an explanation as to why will be left to a little later. Second, a name has had to be devised for the first sequenced component, FILE BODY, because the data description of the file does not include a description of this part of the data. A fairly common name used by JSP users for the major child component (i.e. biggest part) of a sequence is the 'body'.

The process of refinement then continues by attempting to refine each child component produced from the previous level of refinement, and so on until further refinement is not significant. In the case of Example 3.2 only one further level of refinement is necessary, as in Figure 3.12.

A question to be answered is, 'When do you stop the process of refinement?' The process of refinement should stop for a particular component when either it would not be sensible to refine the component or the branch of the data structure

arising from the component would not include any iterations or selections. Examples of the latter might be a record which if refined would only lead to a sequence of items, or a report page which if refined would only lead to a sequence of lines consisting of a heading line followed by three different total lines.

Before we finish with Example 3.2, we should investigate the alternative solution suggested for the refinement of the root component, UNSORTED TRANSACTION FILE, as an iteration of 'record'. If this solution were adopted the complete data structure derived would be as shown in Figure 3.13. This solution is wrong because it suggests that *any* record could be a DATA RECORD or an END-OF-FILE RECORD, whereas the data description says that the last record *only* is an END-OF-FILE RECORD and all preceding records are DATA RECORDs.

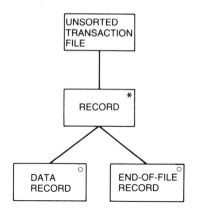

Figure 3.13   *Wrong refinement for Example 3.2*

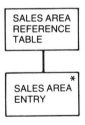

Figure 3.15   *Sales area reference table data structure*

Before concluding this section a number of worked examples will be given.

Example 3.3   *Sales area reference table*
A sales area reference table held internally within primary storage consists of twenty entries. Each entry contains two items, a unique sales area code and a sales area name.

A picture of an instance of the table, with the progress of refinement documented alongside, is

given in Figure 3.14. The resulting data structure would be represented as a JSP data structure diagram as in Figure 3.15.

Example 3.4   *Sorted transactions file*
A sorted transaction file consists of a set of data records, all of the same type, terminated by an end-of-file record. There may be instances where two or more adjacent records have the same key.

A picture of an instance of the file, with the progress of refinement documented alongside, is given in Figure 3.16 (overleaf).
    The resulting data structure would be represented as a JSP data structure diagram as in Figure 3.17 (overleaf).

Example 3.5   *Stock movements file*
A stock movements file consists of a set of data records, sorted into part number sequence. Each data record may be one of two types, representing either an issue of a part from stock or a receipt of a part into stock. There may be more than one data record with the same part number. The data records are terminated by an end-of-file record.

A picture of an instance of the file, together with the progress of refinement, is given in Figure 3.18 (overleaf). The resulting data structure would be represented as a JSP data structure diagram as in Figure 3.19 (overleaf).

	SALES AREA ENTRY	02	S. London
	SALES AREA ENTRY	03	N. London
SALES AREA REFERENCE TABLE	SALES AREA ENTRY	05	Bedfordshire
	SALES AREA ENTRY	07	Buckinghamshire
	SALES AREA ENTRY	09	Hertfordshire
	SALES AREA ENTRY	10	Essex
	ETC.		

Zeroth level   First level
of refinement   of refinement

Figure 3.14   *Refinement of sales area reference table*

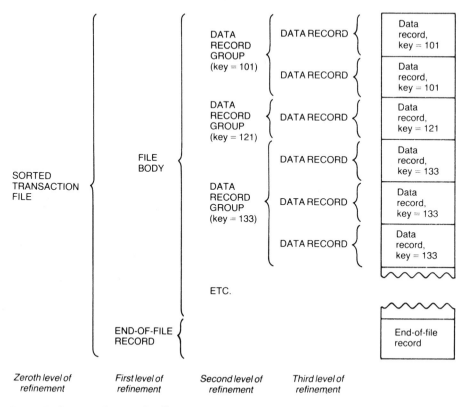

Figure 3.16   *Refinement of transaction file*

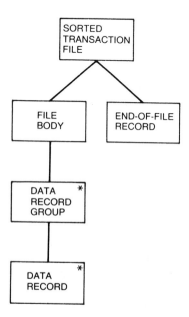

Figure 3.17   *Transaction file data structure*

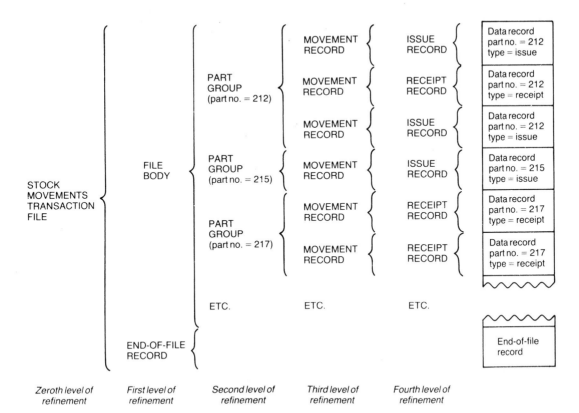

Figure 3.18 *Refinement of stock movements transaction file*

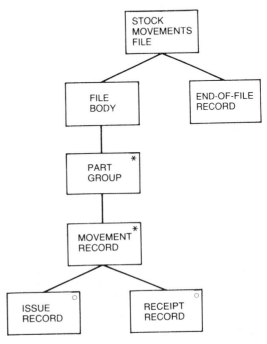

Figure 3.19 *Stock movements transaction file data structure*

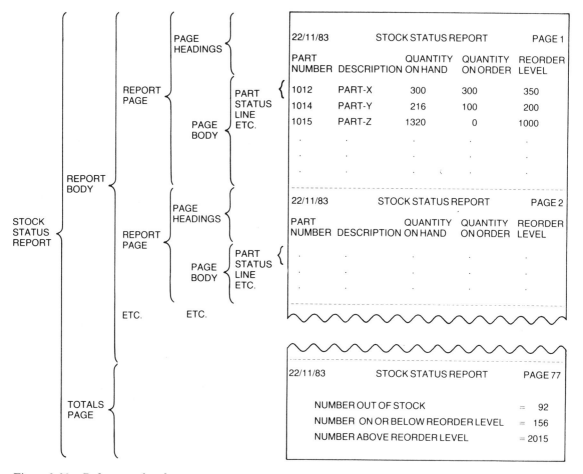

Figure 3.20   *Refinement of stock status report*

Example 3.6   *Stock status report*

A stock status report is produced on a printer. It is a paged report containing headings at the top of each page; the headings include the title of the report, the date and page number. The last page of the report further contains a three-line report identifying the total number of parts whose quantity on hand is zero (i.e. out of stock), on or below reorder level, or above reorder level. The remaining pages further contain for each part a one-line stock status summary including the following items: part number, description of part, quantity on hand, quantity on order and reorder level. Each of these pages contains twenty-five stock status lines, except the last which may contain from one to twenty-five such lines.

A rough picture of an instance of such a report, together with the progress of refinement, is given in Figure 3.20.

The resulting data structure would be represented as a JSP data structure diagram as in Figure 3.21.

Example 3.7   *Customer name and address file*

A customer name and address file consists of a set of records, one per customer, terminated by an end-of-file record. Each record is of variable

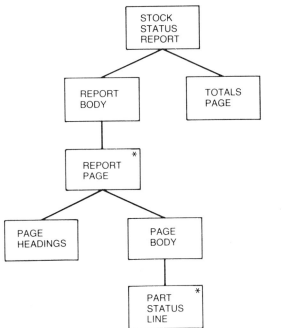

Figure 3.21   *Stock status report data structure*

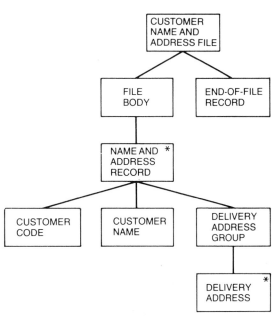

Figure 3.22   *Name and address file data structure*

length, containing a customer code, customer name, and up to ten delivery addresses.

This is an example of a data file whose data structure will need to be taken to below record level, i.e. to item level, because an iteration of an item (delivery address) is involved. The JSP data structure diagram for this file is shown in Figure 3.22.

Physical versus logical data structures

The starting point for producing a data structure is a description of the data whose structure is required. A little more needs to be said about the nature of this description before concluding this chapter. A fundamental assumption of JSP is that the data description used and hence the data structure produced should represent the program's view of that data, i.e. should include all, and only, the characteristics of the data important to the program.

Ingevaldsson[2] describes such a data structure as a 'logical' data structure. He further describes the structure that exhaustively covers all the characteristics of the data as seen by any program as the 'physical' data structure. By his definition therefore the majority of the data structures produced so far are physical data structures, because they have been produced from descriptions of data independent of any particular program which may process that data. The data structures referred to in the first step of the JSP method are logical data structures, and from now on any reference to data structures relates to logical data structures unless explicitly identified as physical. The concept of logical data structures is best illustrated with a few examples.

Order record C=1012 S = 11	Order record C=1012 S = 11	Order record C=1014 S = 11	Order record C=1253 S = 13	Order record C=1999 S = 16	Order record C=1999 S = 16	Order record C=1999 S = 16	Order record C= 2009 S = 16		End-of-file record

where C is customer number, S is sales area

Figure 3.23   *Picture of the orders file*

Example 3.8   *Orders file*
An orders file contains a collection of order records, each order record representing an order from a customer for a part. The order records are in sequence of customer number within sales area number. The order records are terminated by an end-of-file record.

A picture of an instance of the file is given in Figure 3.23.

If the program which is being designed is going to input the orders file and produce a report of the number of orders per customer and per sales area,

then the programmer will be interested in the fact that the order records are grouped by customer and that customer groups are further grouped by sales area. In this situation the programmer would produce the data structure diagram in Figure 3.24.

However, if the program is to input the orders file and produce a report of the number of orders per customer, then the fact that order records are grouped by sales area would be of no interest and the data structure diagram in Figure 3.25 would be produced.

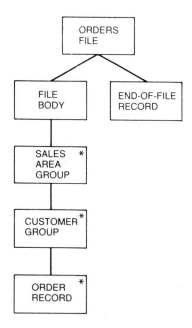

Figure 3.24   *One view of the orders file*

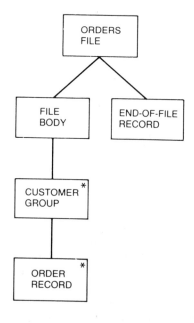

Figure 3.25   *Alternative view of the orders file*

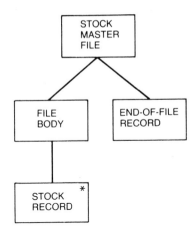

Figure 3.26   *One view of stock master file*

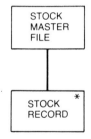

Figure 3.27   *Alternative view of stock master file*

Example 3.9   *Indexed sequential stock file*
An indexed sequential stock master file held on magnetic disk contains stock records in logical sequence of part number key, terminated by an end-of-file record. Each stock record has a unique part number key.

If this master file is to be processed sequentially from the beginning to the end of the file, then the data structure diagram that represents the correct view of the file is as given in Figure 3.26.

If however the master file is to be processed selectively (i.e. randomly), then the data structure diagram that represents the correct view of the file is as given in Figure 3.27.

The reason for the difference between these two data structure diagrams is that sequential processing requires that the end of the file be detected, so that the processing program knows that it has processed all the records in the file, whereas in random processing this condition can not arise.

One way of ensuring that the data description used, and hence the data structure produced, represents the program's view of the data, is to simulate the detailed processing of the program using some simple data. This will help you identify the characteristics of the data important to the program.

One further point concerns the refinement of data below record level. Normally the process of refinement will not require the refinement of data below record level except when iterations and/or selections of data items are involved. When refinement does occur below record level the order in which sequenced components representing data items is specified is not significant. The reason for this is that once a record has been read into primary storage the data items can be accessed in any order and also accessed many times. This means that in a logical data structure a record's data items may be presented in a sequence which is convenient for processing by the program. Furthermore, because a program may access a data item more than once a particular data item may be required to be included more than once in the record's structure. To illustrate the former situation, consider if the stock record of Example 3.9 contains, in the physical order specified, the following data items: stock item number, stock item name, item price, quantity on hand, quantity on order and reorder level. If each stock record is to be processed by a program which identifies those records whose quantity on hand has fallen below reorder level, then the part of the logical data structure representing the structure of the record is as in Figure 3.28 (overleaf). The data structure in Figure 3.28 could be simplified by grouping the data items represented by components 2, 3 and 4 together in one data component. Furthermore, if the particular program in question does not process, say, item price and quantity on order, then these data items may be omitted from the logical data structure.

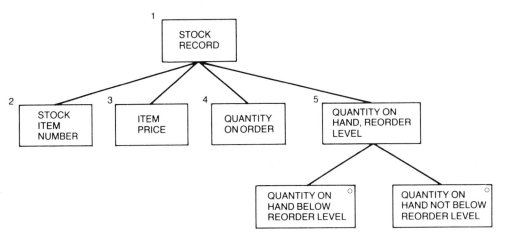

Figure 3.28   *Logical data structure for stock record*

Interactive I/O data structures

More and more of the data processing systems being developed or redeveloped have some programs which interact directly with human beings, i.e. users. These programs are called 'interactive' programs to distinguish them from 'batch' programs. Batch programs input their non-master data (usually transaction data) from pre-stored data contained in files on secondary storage, whereas interactive programs input their non-master data direct from the user keying in the data at a terminal (e.g. a VDU). The examples of transaction data input, and their respective JSP data structures that have been looked at so far (in Examples 3.1, 3.2, 3.4, 3.5 and 3.8, for instance), have been for batch programs.

There are some important differences between interactive programs and batch programs which affect the derivation of the data structures for the design of a program using JSP. These are discussed under heading (a)–(c) below.

(a) Prompting for data

The transaction data for a batch program will have been batched and stored in a file prior to the execution of the program. During the execution of the program, the program helps itself to the transaction data from the file, record by record, until it reaches the end-of-file record.

An interactive program, on the other hand, receives its transaction data, record by record and data item by data item, direct from the user keying in the data at a terminal. In order that the user knows when and what data to input the program needs to prompt the user with an output message at the terminal, informing the user when and what data is required. Hence the input of transaction data to an interactive program always involves a dialogue or conversation between the program and the user at a terminal. The dialogue consists of an alternation of program output prompt followed by user input. This dialogue continues until the user keys in input indicating the termination of transaction data. Such a dialogue can be expressed as a JSP data structure, as illustrated by Example 3.10.

Example 3.10   *Customer orders dialogue*

An interactive program accepts customer orders keyed in at a terminal. Each customer order consists of the following data items:

customer number (5 alphanumeric characters)

order number (2 alphabetic characters followed by 4 numeric digits)
number of items in order (3 numeric digits)
and for each stock item in order:
stock item number (1 alphabetic character followed by 3 numeric digits)
quantity required (4 numeric digits)

After each customer order the program asks if there are any more customer orders to input. A negative response terminates the program.

A picture of an example dialogue for this program, assuming all data input is valid, is given in Figure 3.29. In the picture, program output messages/prompts are indicated in lower-case italic and user input is shown in upper case. Also shown in Figure 3.29 is the progress of refinement for producing the resulting JSP data structure given in Figure 3.30 (overleaf). Note that in

Figure 3.30 the data components ORDER HEADER, ITEM ORDER and ORDER END could be refined further as sequences, although it is not necessary. ORDER END, for instance, could be refined as in Figure 3.31 (overleaf).

(b) Validation of data

If a batch program is responsible for validating the transaction data it inputs, then errors in the data are highlighted in a report produced during the execution of the program. This report is not made available to the user until some time after the execution of the program is complete. Then, and only then, can corrections to the data be initiated, leading to the corrected data being input to a re-run of the program.

An interactive program, on the other hand, can validate the transaction data, item by item and record by record, as it is keyed in by the user. The

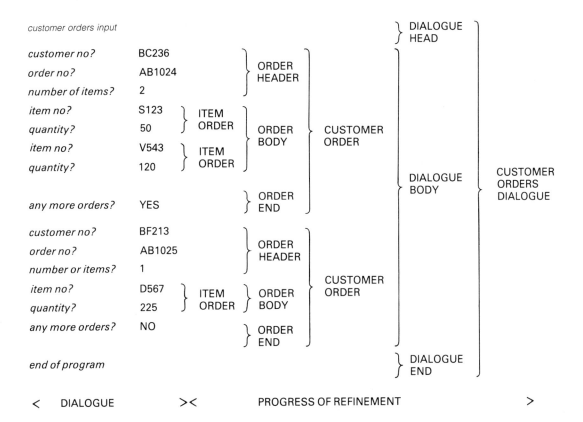

Figure 3.29 *Customer orders dialogue without validation*

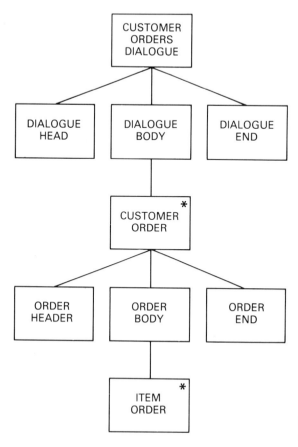

Figure 3.30   *Customer orders dialogue data structure*

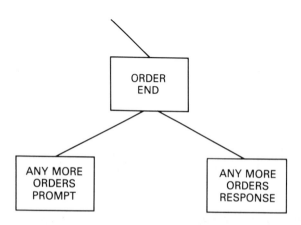

Figure 3.31   *Possible refinement of ORDER END from Figure 3.30*

Customer orders input

customer no?	BC23
too short, please try again	
customer no?	BC236
order no?	AB1024
number of items?	2
item no?	SX23
invalid, please try again	
item no?	1234
invalid, please try again	
item no?	S123
quantity?	120
item no?	V543

.
.
.

any more orders?	HELP
invalid response, please try again	
any more orders?	NO

end of program

Figure 3.32   *Extract from customer orders dialogue with validation*

program can respond to the user immediately when invalid data is input and output a request to the user to re-input with, it is hoped, valid data. The interactive dialogue therefore not only consists of program output prompts for user input and data input by the user but also, potentially, program output messages indicating invalid data and program output prompts requesting re-input of data.

The impact of data validation on an interactive dialogue is illustrated in Figure 3.32 where the impact on only part of the dialogue is shown. Figure 3.33 gives the JSP data structure for this revised dialogue. Note in particular that the data structure must take into account that for every user input there may be 0, 1 or more invalid inputs entered by the user before a valid input is accepted by the program.

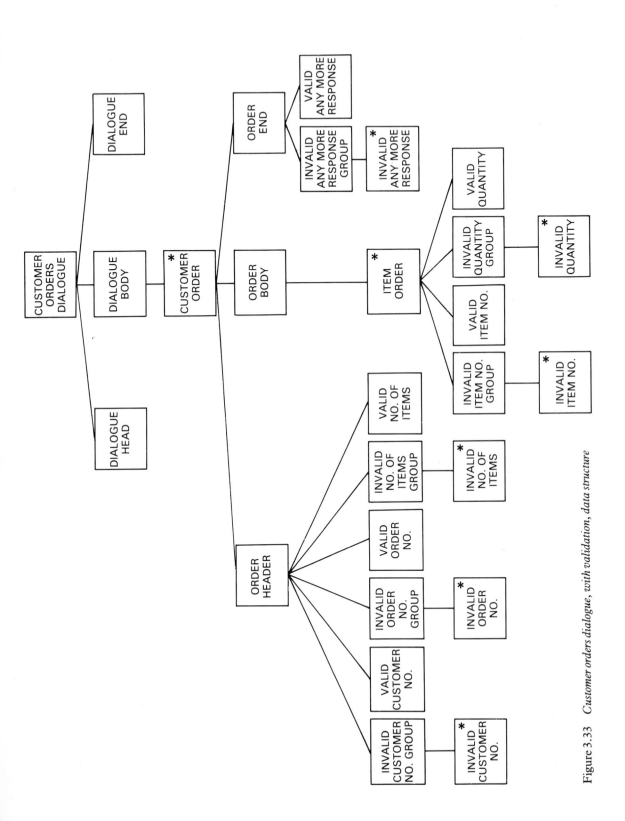

Figure 3.33 *Customer orders dialogue, with validation, data structure*

(c) Reporting on results

A batch program can only communicate its results of processing to users via a printed report made available to the user sometime after the execution of the program is complete.

However, in the case of interactive programs low-volume results can be output to the user as and when they have been produced by the program as part of the interactive dialogue.

Exercises

3.1 *Batched card file*
A card file is made up of batches of cards. Each batch has a header card and any number of detail cards following the header card. The file is terminated by an end-of-file card.
   Produce the JSP physical data structure diagram for the card file.

3.2 *Variable-length customer record*
A variable-length customer record contains a customer code, customer name, customer address and discount data in that order. The discount data is either a single discount code or a list of one or more percentages.
   Produce the JSP physical data structure diagram for the customer record.

3.3 *Invoice file*
An invoice file consists of a number of invoice records terminated by an end-of-file record. The records are sorted by date within customer number.
   Produce the JSP physical data structure diagram for the invoice file.

3.4 *Customer name and address file*
A validated file contains customer names and addresses. Each customer is represented by one or two records. The first record contains the customer's account number, the record type (1, to indicate first record), the customer's name and the first and second lines of the address. The second record, if required, contains the customer's account number, the record type (2, to indicate second record) and the third, fourth and fifth lines of the address. The file is terminated by an end-of-file record.
   Produce the JSP physical data structure

diagram for the file.

3.5 *Stock movements file*
Produce a revised JSP physical data structure diagram for the stock movements file in Example 3.5, assuming that the records are sorted into record type (receipts before issues) within part number sequence.

3.6 *Multitype record file*
A validated serial file contains data records of two types (type 1 and type 2). The file is terminated by an end-of-file record.
   (a) Produce the JSP logical data structure, assuming the file is to be processed by a program which is to count the total number of records in the file.
   (b) Produce the JSP logical data structure, assuming the file is to be processed by a program which counts how many type 1 records and how many type 2 records are in the file.

3.7 *Personnel file*
A validated personnel file contains one data record per employee. A data record contains:
   employee code
   employee name
   department code
   grade
   years of service
   attendance (days worked)
   salary.
The file is in employee code within department code sequence and terminated by an end-of-file record.
   Produce the JSP logical data structure for the personnel file for each of the following three programs:

(a)   A program which prints the name and years of service for all employees whose years of service is greater than X;

(b)   A program which prints the total yearly salary bill for each department;

(c)   A program which calculates the holidays for each employee using the following algorithm:

Grades 1–3

Three or fewer years of service	allow fifteen days for holidays
Four to ten years of service	allow twenty days for holidays
Over ten years of service	allow twenty-five days for holidays

Grades 4–6

Three or fewer years of service	allow twenty days for holidays
Four to ten years of service	allow twenty-five days for holidays
Over ten years of service	allow thirty days for holidays

3.8   *Interactive I/O of stock issue transactions*
An on-line program inputs stock issue transactions from a terminal. Each stock issue transaction consists of a part number followed by a quantity issued. The program prompts the terminal operator for each data item value and validates each data item value as it is input. If an item value is found to be invalid the program rejects it immediately, displays an appropriate error message for the operator and requests the re-input of the item value. To terminate the input of transactions the operator types in a zero part number. Produce the JSP data structure for the interactive I/O dialogue.

4 Producing a preliminary program structure 1

When the data structures associated with a program have been produced, the next step in the JSP method is to derive a first, or preliminary, version of the program structure from these data structures. This chapter concentrates on programs with one or two data structures, leaving the extra problems associated with programs involving more than two data structures to the next chapter of the book.

The first section of this chapter examines the relationship between the preliminary program structure and its associated data structures, demonstrating that each program component has a direct relationship with a data component in one or more of the data structures.

The second section provides an introduction to the process of producing the preliminary program structure by concentrating on the rare situation of a program with a single data structure.

The third and fourth sections of the chapter then turn to the more complicated process of producing the preliminary structure of a program with two data stuctures.

The relationship between a program structure and its data structures

As explained in Chapter 2, a fundamental principle of the JSP method is that the structure of a program should be based upon the structures of the data processed by the program. What this actually means is that for each part of the data to be processed by the program, i.e. for each data component contained in the data structures, there should be a corresponding program component within the program structure which can be identified as responsible for processing that part of the data. This important concept will be illustrated with an example.

Example 4.1 *Payments summary program*
A customer payments file on magnetic tape contains a collection of records, each record representing a payment made by a customer. The payment records are in customer number sequence and terminated by an end-of-file record. There may be more than one payment record per customer. A program is required to input the records from this file and produce a payments summary report. This report is unpaged, containing headings at the top of the report followed by one detail line for each customer within the customer payments file. Each customer detail line contains the customer number and the total of all payments made by that customer.

There are two data structures involved with this program, namely those in Figure 4.1 (the verification of these two structures is left to the reader). The preliminary program structure that would be derived from these data structures using the JSP method would be as in Figure 4.2 (no attempt will be made, at this stage, to explain how it was derived).

Each component within the two data structures represents a part of the data which is to be processed by the program. For instance, component 4 in the customer payments file represents a group of payment records for a customer that is to be input by the program and processed to produce the total payment for that customer. Similarly each component within the program structure represents part of the program which eventually will be translated into a set of programming language statements responsible for carrying out part of the total processing function of the program. A principle of JSP is that each data component should have a corresponding program component, i.e. that for each part of the data there should be a clearly identifiable part of the program whose responsibility it is to wholly process that data.

This can be verified for Example 4.1 by comparing the two data structures in Figure 4.1

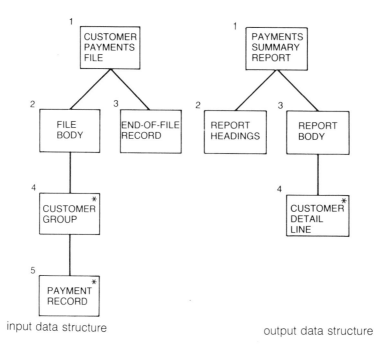

input data structure

output data structure

Figure 4.1   *Data structures for payments summary program*

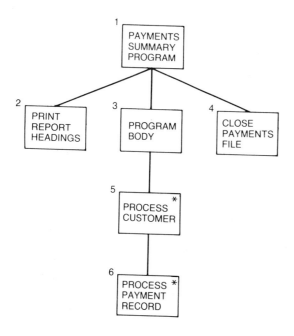

Figure 4.2   *Preliminary program structure for payments summary program*

with the program structure in Figure 4.2. Each component within the input data structure represents input data which is wholly processed by a component within the program structure. Similarly each component within the output data structure represents output data which is wholly produced by a component within the program structure. For instance the program component PROCESS CUSTOMER will input a CUSTOMER GROUP of payment records and output a CUSTOMER DETAIL LINE for that customer. All the relationships between the data and program components of Example 4.1 are summarized in Figure 4.3 and illustrated using the structure diagrams in Figure 4.4. These structure diagrams have been deliberately drawn in a non-standard way in order to emphasize the relationships between components more clearly. What Figure 4.4 clearly demonstrates is that every data component can be related to one, and only one, program component and that each program component in the preliminary program structure is related to one, and only one, input data component and/or output data component.

The other relationship that can be seen between

the data structures and the program structure is that if the two data structures are 'matched' together, then the program structure has the same 'shape' as the matched data structures. A characteristic of the shape is the relationship of parent to child components, i.e. sequence, selection or iteration. The matched data structures may be obtained by adding 'dummy' components to each data structure so that each program component has two corresponding data components, one from each of the two data structures and one, and only one, of which may be a dummy component. This is illustrated in Figure 4.5 (overleaf), where the same underlying shape of the program structure and the two matched data structures is obvious (the dummy components are highlighted by using broken lines).

Input data component	Program component	Output data component
1 Customer payments file	1 Payments summary program	1 Payments summary report
—	2 Print report headings	2 Report headings
2 File body	3 Program body	3 Report body
3 End-of-file record	4 Close payments file	—
4 Customer group	5 Process customer	4 Customer detail line
5 Payment record	6 Process payment record	—

Figure 4.3 *Summary of relationships between data and program components for payments summary program*

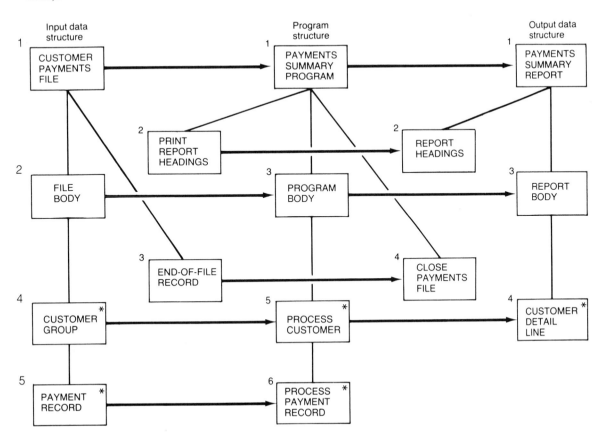

Figure 4.4 *Relationship between data and program structures for payments summary program*

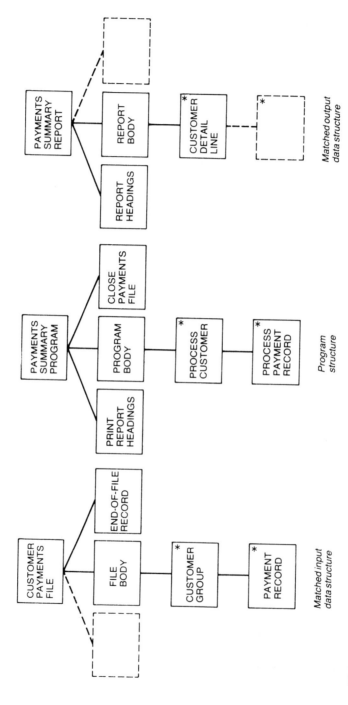

Figure 4.5   *Relationship between matched data structures and program structure for payments summary program*

The remaining sections of this chapter will explain how the preliminary program structure may be derived from its data structures.

Programs based on a single data structure

The simplest programs, from the point of view of JSP, are those whose structure is wholly determined by a single data structure. Although programs of this nature are rare they are worth considering at this stage because they provide an easy introduction to the process of producing the preliminary program structure from the data structures.

Example 4.2   *Times table program*
A program is required to produce all 'times tables' from 1 to 12. Each times table is to be printed on a separate printer page with a heading identifying the particular times table. The only data involved with this program is the output, i.e. the printed times tables, and its data structure is given in Figure 4.6.

As each program component must correspond to a data component within one or more of its associated data structures, and there is only one data structure associated with this particular program, then the components of the program structure must correspond one for one with those of the data structure. Furthermore, the shape of the program structure is exactly that of the data structure. Hence the program structure has exactly the same structure as the data structure in Figure 4.6, and differs only in terms of the component names which, in the case of the program structure, define the precise function of each component in the program. Figure 4.7 (overleaf) gives the program structure for the times table program and shows its correspondence with the data structure of Figure 4.6.

Hence producing the preliminary program structure for a program involving only one data structure is reasonably straightforward. Life is seldom so easy!

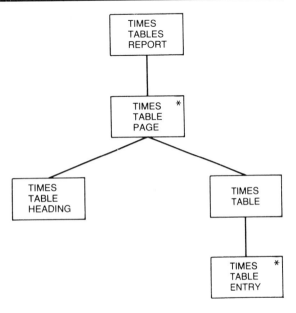

Figure 4.6   *Data structure for times table report*

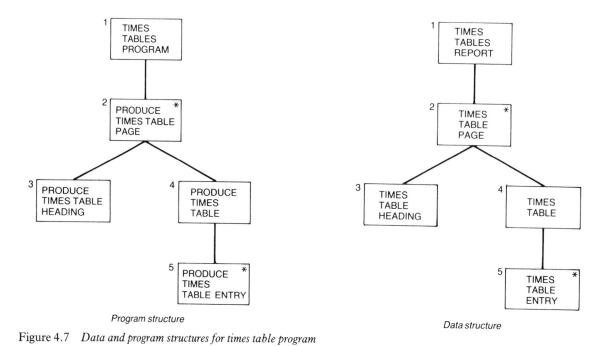

Figure 4.7   *Data and program structures for times table program*

Programs based on two data structures

The process of producing the preliminary program structure for a program involving two data structures, usually an input and an output, is more complicated than that for a program involving a single data structure. The process can be broken down into three steps:

1   Identify correspondences between components in the two data structures.
2   Produce 'matched' data structure diagrams.
3   Produce preliminary program structure.

The process will now be explained and illustrated using Example 4.1, the payments summary program. The starting point is of course the two data structure diagrams from Figure 4.1, which are repeated in Figure 4.8.

The first step is to identify correspondences between the components of one data structure and the components of the other data structure. Putting it another way, in relation to the two data structures in Figure 4.8, each component in the

input data structure should be examined in turn and the question asked:

> If an instance of this data component is processed completely by the program, is there an instance of a data component in the output data structure which is wholly produced?

If such a component is identified, there is a correspondence between this output data component and the input data component.

There are some rules which will help you to correctly identify correspondences.

Rules for identifying correspondence
1   Your method of working should be to take each input data component in turn, starting with the root component and progressively working down the structure until the lowest-level component(s) have been considered. Furthermore, in considering data components on the same level you should work from the

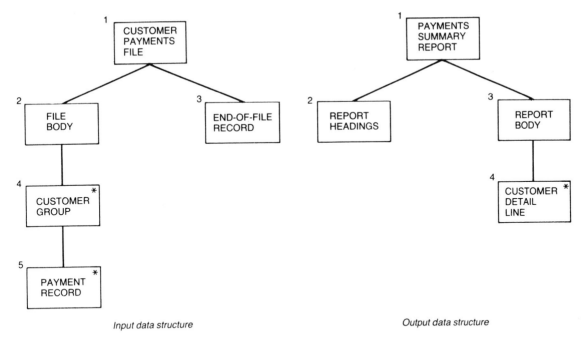

Input data structure   Output data structure

Figure 4.8   *Data structures for payments summary program*

Input data structure

No.	Data component name	No. of instances
1	Customer payments file	1
2	File body	1
3	End-of-file record	1
4	Customer group	No. of customers
5	Payment record	No. of payment records

Output data structure

No.	Data component name	No. of instances
1	Payments summary report	1
2	Report headings	1
3	Report body	1
4	Customer detail line	No. of customers

Figure 4.9   *Number of instances of components within data structures for payments summary program*

leftmost to the rightmost. For example, the order in which you would consider the input data components in Figure 4.8 is 1, 2, 3, 4 and 5.

2   A component in one data structure may have no or one only corresponding component in the other data structure.

3   Corresponding data components should have the same number of instances in each of their data structures and must occur in the same order. To prepare yourself for the process of identifying correspondences it might help you to explicitly identify the number of instances of each data component in each data structure. Figure 4.9 gives these instances for the two data structures in Figure 4.8. What these tables tell us is that: input data component 1 might correspond with output data component 1 or 2 or 3, and similarly input data components 2 and 3; input data component 4 can correspond with output component 4; and input component 5 cannot possibly correspond with any output data component.

4 An input data component cannot correspond with an output data component at a higher level in the output data structure than an already corresponded output data component. For instance the situation in Figure 4.10 cannot happen.
5 When sequenced components in the input data structure are corresponded with sequenced components in the output data structure, an input data component may be only corresponded with an output data component to the right of already corresponded output data components. For instance the situation in Figure 4.11 cannot happen.

However, this rule does *not* apply when sequenced components are corresponded which represent data items because, as explained in Chapter 3, the data items of a record may be accessed in any order and as many times as required. Hence the order of the data items of a record contained in a logical data structure does not necessarily indicate that they have to be processed in that order.
6 When selected components in the input data structure are corresponded with selected components in the output data structure, an input data component may be corresponded with *any* output data component. For instance the situation in Figure 4.12 is allowed.

If these rules are followed, the correspondences summarized in Figure 4.13 would be identified for the components in the two data structures of Figure 4.8.

You should note that the input data components END-OF-FILE RECORD and PAYMENT RECORD do not have any corresponding output data components because as a result of processing an instance of these two data components no output, identifiable as components in the output data structure, is produced. Similarly the output data component REPORT HEADINGS has no corresponding

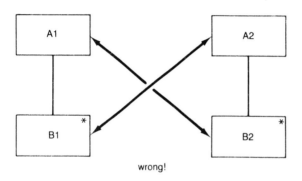

Figure 4.10 *Disallowed data component correspondences*

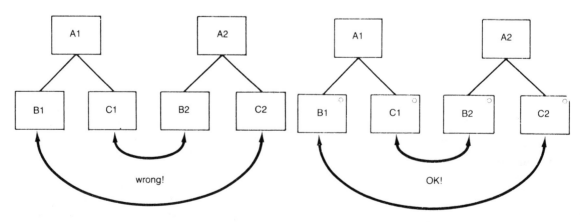

Figure 4.11 *Disallowed correspondences with sequenced components*

Figure 4.12 *Allowed correspondences with selected components*

Input data component		If completely processed will produce	Output data component	
No.	Name		No.	Name
1	Customer payments file	→	1	Payments summary report
2	File body	→	3	Report body
4	Customer group	→	4	Customer detail line

Figure 4.13 *Correspondences between data components of payments summary program*

input data component because no input data needs to be processed in order to produce an instance of this data component.

The correspondences can be illustrated using the two data structure diagrams as in Figure 4.14.

Before moving on to the next step of the process you should note that corresponding components in Figure 4.14 happen to be of the same type, i.e. both are sequenced or selected or iterated components. However, situations could arise where this is not true, and this is discussed in the next section.

Now that the correspondences between components in the two data structures have been identified, the next step is to produce 'matched' data structures, i.e. structures that have the same shape. As a result of identifying correspondences each data component has either one or no corresponding component. The process of 'matching' the data structures involves introducing 'dummy' components into the two data structures so that all data components have a corresponding component, in some cases perhaps a dummy component. This would result for Example 4.1 in the two matched data structures shown in Figure 4.15 (overleaf). The empty boxes with broken lines represent the dummy components. As the reader can confirm, the introduction of these dummy components has not invalidated the original data structures.

A particular characteristic of the matched data structures is that corresponding components now occupy the same physical positions within the two structures. In producing matched data structures which involve selections or sequences of data items, some reordering of the selected or sequenced components may be necessary so that

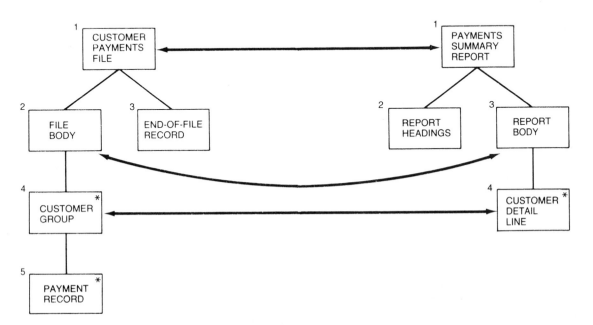

Figure 4.14 *Correspondences between data structures for payments summary program*

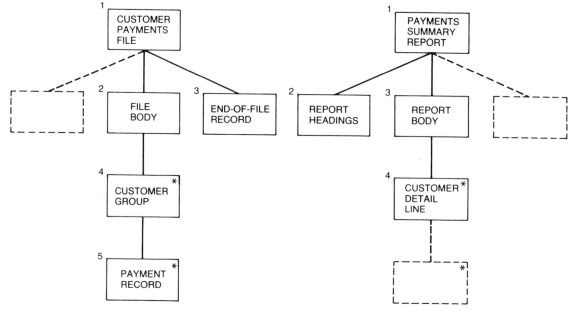

Figure 4.15 *Matched data structures for payments summary program*

this is true. For example, a reordering of components B1 and C1, or alternatively B2 and C2, would be necessary in producing matched data structures involving the selections in Figure 4.12. It should be remembered that the order of selected components in a data or program structure is not significant except when optimizing a program (see Chapter 12).

What has been achieved by the matching process is that the underlying shape of the program has been identified because it is represented by the common shape of the two matched data structures. Hence in the case of Example 4.1 the shape (or skeleton) of the program structure is as illustrated in Figure 4.16.

What remains to be done in the process of producing the preliminary program structure is to identify the function of each program component in the skeleton structure and provide suitable concise, but as precise as possible, names.

It is relatively easy to identify the function of each program component. First, you should remind yourself of the input and/or output data

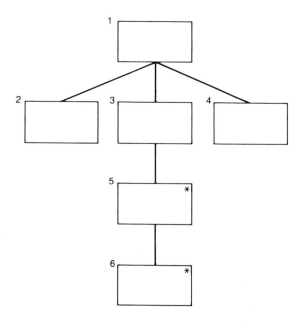

Figure 4.16 *Skeleton program structure for payments summary program*

Program component no.	Corresponding input data component	Corresponding output data component
1	Customer payments file	Payments summary report
2	——	Report headings
3	File body	Report body
4	End-of-file record	——
5	Customer group	Customer detail line
6	Payment record	——

Figure 4.17 *Corresponding data and program components for payments summary program*

Program component number	Description of function
1	Process customer payments file to produce payments summary report
2	Process report headings
3	Process file body to produce report body
4	Process end-of-file record
5	Process customer group to produce customer detail line
6	Process payment record

Figure 4.18 *Function of each program component for payments summary program*

components which correspond to each component in the skeleton program structure. For Example 4.1 this is summarized in Figure 4.17.

A description of the function of each program component name can be obtained either, for a program component with corresponding input and output data components, by including the input and output data component names in the following sentence:

$$PROCESS \ldots TO \, PRODUCE \ldots$$

> input   output
>
> data component name

or, for a program component with only one input or output data component, by including the data component name in the following sentence:

$$PROCESS \ldots$$

> data component name

Therefore for Example 4.1 the function of each program component shown in Figure 4.16 is presented in Figure 4.18.

One problem that many programmers have is to translate these relatively long descriptions of the function of each program component into concise, but meaningful, program component names. Careful thought is required in order that names eventually chosen convey concisely the true function of each program component.

The corresponding preliminary program structure for the payments summary program is that already given in Figure 4.2.

Correspondences between data components of different types

A situation that can arise when matching data structures is that a component in one structure corresponds with a component in another structure of a different type, where type means sequenced, iterated or selected. How this situation is resolved when matching the affected data structures is best illustrated with an example. The example chosen is a simplified version of Example 2.1.

Example 4.3 *Simplified version of demerge program*

A *validated* input sequential file contains two types of record, the type being identified by the character 1 or 2 in the first character position of the record. The input file is terminated by an end-of-file record.

A program is required to input the records from this file and output all type 1 records to one

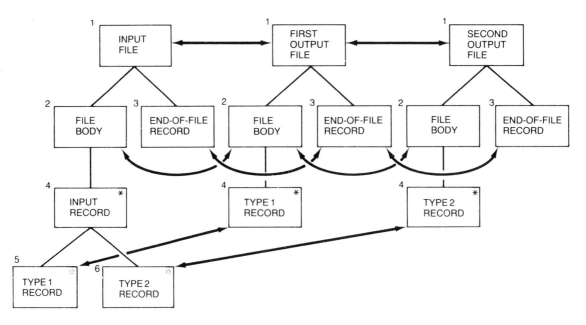

Figure 4.19   *Data structures with correspondences for simplified demerge program*

output file and all type 2 records to a second output file. Both output files should be in the same key sequence as the input file and each should be terminated by an end-of-file record. Only records of type 1 or 2 exist in the input file.

The data structures and component correspondences for this example are depicted in Figure 4.19.

The situation that has arisen is that component 5 in the INPUT FILE, which is a selected component, corresponds to component 4 in the FIRST OUTPUT FILE, which is an iterated component. The same situation has arisen with component 6 in the INPUT FILE and component 4 in the SECOND OUTPUT FILE. This creates a problem in that the final matched data structures must have the same underlying structure, which implies that corresponding components must be of the same type.

The solution to this problem in JSP is to introduce the idea of 'null' components, i.e. absent data, into the matching process. In the case of Example 4.3 the argument would be that, in

processing one INPUT RECORD:

Either one TYPE 1 RECORD would be produced in the FIRST OUTPUT FILE and no record would be produced in the SECOND OUTPUT FILE;
Or no record would be produced in the FIRST OUTPUT FILE and one TYPE 2 RECORD would be produced in the SECOND OUTPUT FILE.

Hence after correspondences have been identified the revised data structures shown in Figure 4.20 would be produced. As it happens these revised data structures exactly match, and the correspondences are implicitly shown by the positions of the components. Component 6 in the FIRST OUTPUT FILE structure and component 5 in the SECOND OUTPUT FILE structure are the null components and represent absent records. The correspondence between each of the components numbered 4 is possible because it can be argued that processing an INPUT RECORD will result in an OUTPUT

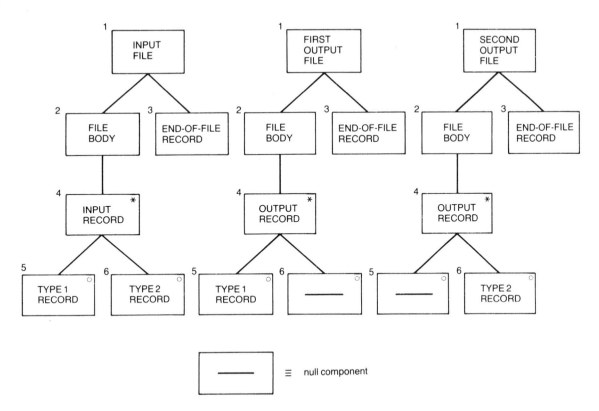

Figure 4.20   *Revised data structures for simplified demerge program*

RECORD, either present or absent, in both output files.

Similar solutions to other similar problems of correspondence between data components of different types can be found.

Exercises

4.1   *Job costing program (first version)*
A job costing file contains one or more validated labour records for each job. Each record contains the following data items:

> Job code
> Grade of employee
> Number of minutes spent by employee on job.

There is one record for each period of time spent by an employee on each job. The records are in sequence of ascending job code and are terminated by an end-of-file record.

A program is to input the job costing file and produce an unpaged job costs summary report containing report headings and a detail line for each job containing the following information:
> Job code
> Total job labour cost

Total job overheads cost.
The report is terminated by an 'end-of-report' message.
The pay for each grade of employee is:
Grade 1: £4.70 per hour
Grade 2: £4.00 per hour
Grade 3: £3.10 per hour.
Overheads are estimated to be £5.00 per labour hour.

The JSP data structures for the two files of this program are given in Figure 4.21.

You are required to:
(a)   Identify the correspondences between the two data structures;
(b)   Produce matched data structures;
(c)   Produce a preliminary program structure.

4.2   *Employees holidays program*
The personnel file described in Exercise 3.7

is to be input by a program which produces an employees holidays report. The report is to be paged, each page containing the details for one department. Each page contains headings, including an identification of the department, and one detail line for each employee in the department containing
Employee code
Employee name
Number of days holiday.
You should assume that each department's employees can fit on to one page.

The data structure for the employees holidays report is given in Figure 4.22.

You are required to:
(a)   Produce the data structure for the personnel file;
(b)   Identify the correspondences between the personnel file data structure and

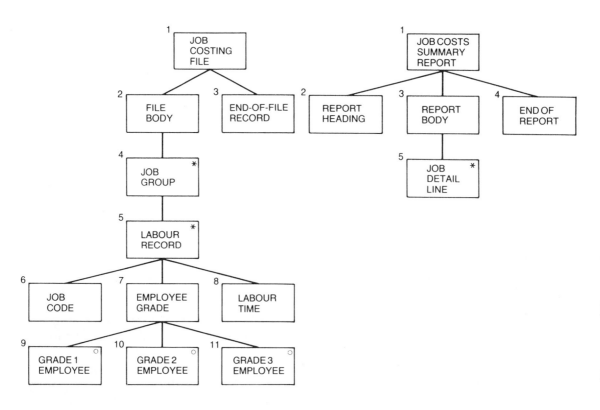

Figure 4.21   *Data structures for job costing program*

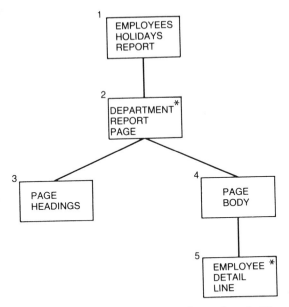

Figure 4.22   *Report data structure for employee holidays program*

the employees holidays report data structure;

(c)   Produce the two matched data structures;

(d)   Produce the preliminary program structure.

In addition:

(e)   What would be the impact on the employees holidays report data structure, and hence the preliminary program structure, if the report on a department could occupy more than one page, assuming a new department always starts on a new page?

4.3   *Job costing program (second version)*

The specification of the validated job costing file of Exercise 4.1 is amended so that it now contains two types of record, labour records and material records. The specification of the labour record additionally contains a record type data item (L, to indicate labour record). A material record contains the following data items:

Record type (M, to indicate a material record)
Job code
Material cost.

There is one material record for each material used on the job. The records in the file are still in ascending sequence of job code.

The program is now required to produce a *paged* job cost summary report with report headings on each page. The detail line for each job should additionally contain the total material cost for the job.

You are required to:

(a)   Produce the revised data structures for the job costing file and the job cost summary report;

(b)   Identify correspondence between the two data structures;

(c)   Produce matched data structures;

(d)   Produce a preliminary program structure.

4.4   *Stock status program*

A sequential stock master file contains one record per stock item. Each record contains the following data items:

Stock item number
Stock item name
Item price
Quantity on hand
Reorder level.

The file is in stock item number sequence and is terminated by an end-of-file record. A program is required to input this file and print an unpaged report with report headings, followed by a report on each stock item whose quantity on hand is below reorder level. The program should also keep a running total of the cost of bringing the stock up to reorder levels, and print out this total cost on the end of the report.

You are required to:

(a)   Produce the data structures for the two files;

(b)   Identify correspondences;

(c)   Produce matched data structures;

(d)   Produce the preliminary program structure.

4.5   *Demerge file program*
This exercise relates to the demerge
program in Example 2.1. The data structure
for the input file was presented in Figure
2.13. The data structures for a simplified
version of the program, specified in
Example 4.2, were presented in Figure 4.20.
    You are required to:
(a)   Produce the data structures for the
      three output files specified in Example
      2.1;
(b)   Identify correspondences between all
      four data structures;
(c)   Produce matched data structures;
(d)   Produce the preliminary program
      structure.

5 Producing a preliminary program structure II

The previous chapter explained how the preliminary program structure for a program associated with one or two data structures could be derived. The procedure for producing a preliminary program structure from three or more data structures is more complicated, especially when two or more of the data structures represent input files processed simultaneously.

The first section of this chapter will concentrate on the general problem of producing matched data structures for three or more data structures by using as an example a program involving only one input data structure. The second section will then investigate the 'collation' problem arising when two or more input data structures are involved and they represent files which are processed simultaneously, such as in an update master file program.

Matching more than two data structures

In Chapter 4 the procedure for matching two data structures was explained. However, if more than two data structures are involved the procedure is a little more complicated. It is best illustrated by example. The situation will be avoided in which two or more of the data structures represent input files that are processed simultaneously; this would introduce the further complication of the 'collating' problem discussed in the second section of this chapter.

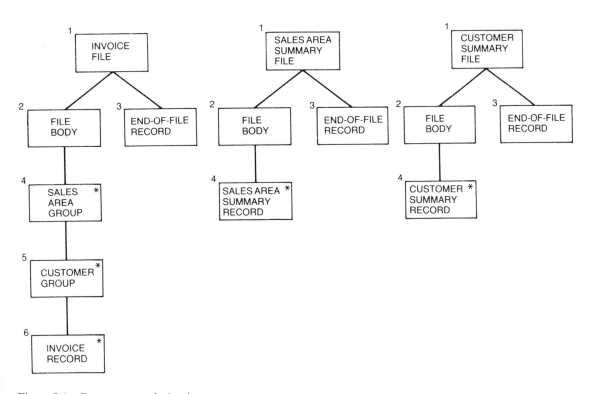

Figure 5.1   *Data structures for invoices summary program*

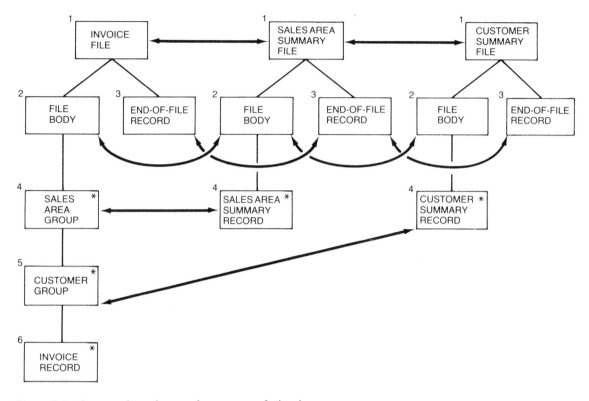

Figure 5.2   *Correspondences between data structures for invoices summary program*

Example 5.1   *Invoices summary program*

An invoice file contains one record per invoice. The invoice records are sorted into customer number within sales area sequence and are terminated by an end-of-file record. There may be more than one record for a particular customer and more than one customer for a sales area. Items included within an invoice record are sales area code, customer number and invoice amount.

The invoice file is to be input, and two output files produced. The first output file is a sales area summary file containing one record per sales area, in sales area code sequence, and terminated by an end-of-file record. Each sales area summary record includes a sales area code and the total of all invoice amounts for that area. The second output file is a customer summary file containing one record per customer, in customer number sequence, and terminated by an end-of-file

record. Each customer summary record includes a customer number and the total of all invoice amounts for that customer.

The three data structures associated with this program are as in Figure 5.1. The first step in producing the preliminary program structure is to identify correspondences between components of the three data structures. The same rules are applied as those described in Chapter 4. However, in this situation there are three data structures, and hence the correspondences should be identified by considering the data structures in pairs. The result of identifying correspondences will be that a particular component in a data structure may have:

A correspondence with a component in each of the other data structures;

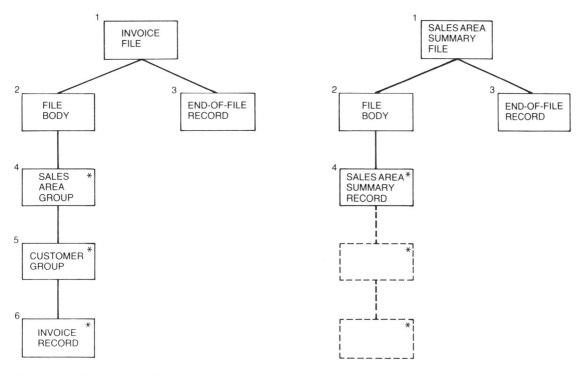

Figure 5.3 *Matched pair of data structures for invoices summary program*

A correspondence with a component in each of a subset of the other data structures;
Or no corresponding components at all.

For example, the resulting correspondences for Example 5.1, shown in Figure 5.2, identify that the FILE BODY components in each of the data structures all correspond, whereas the SALES AREA GROUP component in INVOICE FILE only corresponds with the SALES AREA SUMMARY RECORD component of the SALES AREA SUMMARY FILE, and the INVOICE RECORD component of INVOICE FILE has no corresponding components in either of the other data structures.

The next step in producing the preliminary program structure is to match the data structures. This can be achieved by initially matching two of the data structures. The best two to choose are the input data structure and output data structure that have the most data components associated with them, because this is likely to maximize the degree of matching and hence simplify the remaining steps in the matching procedure when the remaining data structures are included. In the case of Example 5.1 there is only one input data structure, and the two output structures have an equal number of components. The decision as to which two to choose is therefore straightforward for this example; the INVOICE FILE input data structure can be matched with either of the two output data structures, say SALES AREA SUMMARY FILE. The result of matching these two data structures is shown in Figure 5.3.

Having matched two of the data structures, the next step is to introduce a third and match that with the already matched two. During this part of the procedure, dummy components may be added to all three. However, for Example 5.1 the resulting matched data structures, shown in Figure 5.4 (overleaf), indicate that only dummy components are added to the third structure.

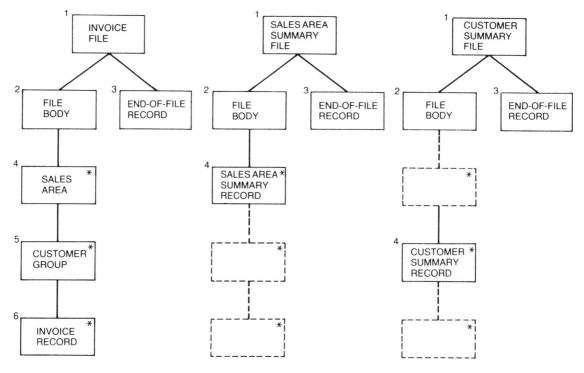

Figure 5.4   *Matched data structures for invoices summary program*

The process of introducing data structures one by one would then continue until they all had been matched. The skeleton program structure would then be the underlying structure of the finally matched data structures, which in the case of Example 5.1 would be as given in Figure 5.5.

The next step in producing the preliminary program structure is the choice of program component names. As explained in Chapter 4, a program component name should be derived from a description of the function of the component, which is itself derived from the names of its associated data component(s). The resulting preliminary program structure for Example 5.1 would be as in Figure 5.6.

The collation problem

A particular problem arises in the formation of a program structure from two or more input data structures when the input files that they represent are processed simultaneously. The latter process is referred to as 'collation' in computing terminology, and hence the problem that arises in the JSP method is referred to as the 'collation problem'. Typical examples of collation are the process of updating a master file with a transaction file or the merging of two files. An internally held reference table processed against one or more input files would itself be treated as an input file and therefore contribute to a collation problem.

The complexity of the solution to the collation problem increases exponentially with the number

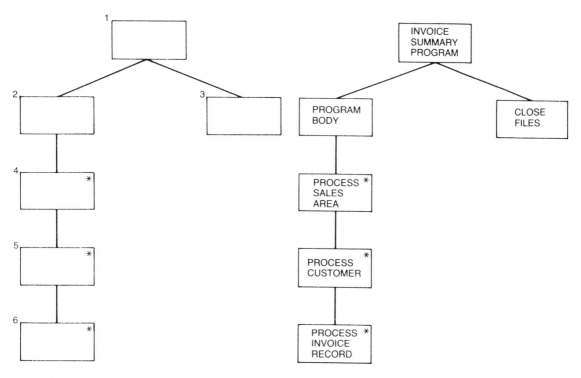

Figure 5.5 *Skeleton program structure for invoices summary program*

Figure 5.6 *Preliminary program structure for invoices summary program*

of input files involved; hence this chapter and book will be restricted to the simplest and most common situation involving only two input data structures, leaving the more complex situations to a more advanced text.

The solution to the collation problem involving two input data structures is best illustrated with an example, a simple merging of two files.

Example 5.2 *Merge program*
Two input files contain records of the same type. Both files are sequentially ordered on the same key and, within each file, each record key is unique. These two files are to be merged to produce a single output file in the same sequence. If a record in the first input file has the same key as a record in the second input file (i.e. 'matches' in data processing terminology, not to be confused with the term 'matched' when referring to data structures) then only the record from the

first input file should be passed to the output file and the record from the second input file should be ignored. Each of the three files is terminated by an end-of-file record.

An example of data contained within the three files is shown in Figure 5.7 (overleaf).

A first attempt at the data structures and component correspondences for this program are as in Figure 5.8 (overleaf).

The collation problem that has arisen is that component 4 in each of the three data structures cannot be corresponded because, as can be seen from the example files in Figure 5.7, the number of instances of FIRST INPUT RECORD is likely to be different from the number of instances of OUTPUT RECORD. With this situation it is impossible to match the three data structures and hence form a program structure.

The solution to this collation problem is to use the idea of absent records introduced in Chapter 4.

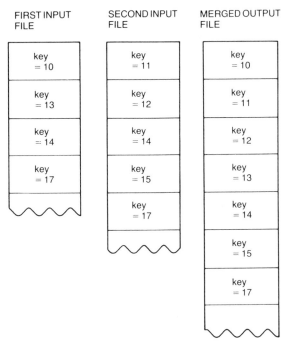

FIRST INPUT FILE   SECOND INPUT FILE   MERGED OUTPUT FILE

Figure 5.7   *Sample data for the three files in merge program*

If the example data files in Figure 5.7 are examined it can be seen that three situations arise:

1   A FIRST INPUT RECORD has a matching SECOND INPUT RECORD.
2   A FIRST INPUT RECORD has no matching SECOND INPUT RECORD, i.e. it matches with an 'absent' SECOND INPUT RECORD.
3   A SECOND INPUT RECORD has no matching FIRST INPUT RECORD, i.e. it matches with an 'absent' FIRST INPUT RECORD.

The example data files in Figure 5.7 are redrawn in Figure 5.9 to take into account this revised 'view' of the data files.

The data structures and correspondences arising from this revised view of the data files are shown in Figure 5.10. It can be seen that component 4 in each of the three data structures can now be corresponded. Furthermore, in the

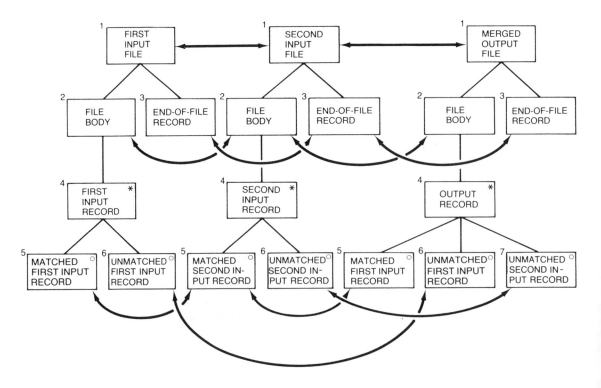

Figure 5.8   *First attempt at data structures and correspondences for merge program*

FIRST INPUT FILE	SECOND INPUT FILE	MERGED OUTPUT FILE
Present record, key = 10	Absent record, key = 10	Present record, key = 10
Absent record, key = 11	Present record, key = 11	Present record, key = 11
Absent record, key = 12	Present record, key = 12	Present record, key = 12
Present record, key = 13	Absent record, key = 13	Present record, key = 13
Present record, key = 14	Present record, key = 14	Present record, key = 14
Absent record, key = 15	Present record, key = 15	Present record, key = 15
Present record, key = 17	Present record, key = 17	Present record, key = 17

case of this example, the three data structures are matched and hence no further manipulation is required to produce the matched data structures. The preliminary program structure that would arise from the matched data structures is depicted in Figure 5.11 (overleaf).

The conclusion arising from this example therefore is that, when considering the data structures for a program involving two or more input files that are processed simultaneously, a view should be taken of all files so that all record keys involved in the processing, whether present or absent in a particular file, are represented in each data structure.

Figure 5.9   *Revised view of data files for merge program*

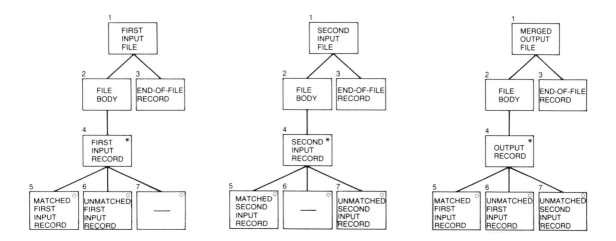

Figure 5.10   *Revised data structures for merge program*

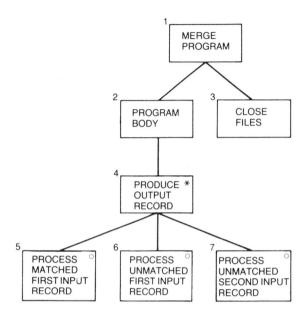

Figure 5.11   *Preliminary program structure for merge program*

Exercises

5.1 *Job costing program (third version)*

This exercise is based upon the job costing file of Exercise 4.3. Amendments to the specification of the job costing file are:

(a) The job cost records are in sequence of record type (labour records before material records) within job code.

(b) The labour record contains the following data items: record type, job code, number of minutes spent by employee on job (the pay for any employee is assumed to be £4.00 per hour).

A program is required to input the job costing file and produce as output a job labour costs file and a job material costs file. The job labour costs file contains one record for each job for which there are one or more labour records in the input file, and each record contains the items job code and job labour cost. The job material costs file contains one record for each job for which there are one or more material records in the input file, and each record contains the items job code and job materials cost. Both output files are in job code sequence, and each is terminated by an end-of-file record.

You are required to:

(a) Produce data structures for the three files;

(b) Identify correspondences;

(c) Produce matched data structures;

(d) Produce a preliminary program structure.

5.2 *Update stock master program (first version)*

The stock master file of Exercise 4.4 is to be updated, by copying, with a stock movements file which contains one record for each issue of an item from stock and contains the data items stock item number and quantity issued. The movements file is in stock item number sequence and is

terminated by an end-of-file record. You
may assume that all movement records have
a matching master record.

You are required to:

(a)   Produce the data structures for the
brought-forward stock master file, the
stock movements file and the carried-
forward stock master file;

(b)   Identify correspondences;

(c)   Produce matched data structures;

(d)   Produce a preliminary program
structure.

5.3   *Update stock master program (second version)*
The specification of the stock movements
file of Exercise 5.2 is amended so that it now
contains two types of record, issue records
and receipt records. The specification of the
issue record additionally contains a record
type data item (I, to indicate issue record). A
receipt record contains data about each
receipt of an item into stock and contains the
following data items: record type (R), stock
item number and quantity received.
Furthermore it is possible that a movement
record has no matching master record, in
which case it should be displayed in an
unpaged error report which will contain
report headings followed by a list of
unmatched movement records.

You are required to:

(a)   Produce the data structures for the
brought-forward stock master file, the
stock movements file, the carried-
forward stock master file and error
report;

(b)   Identify correspondences;

(c)   Produce matched data structures;

(d)   Produce a preliminary program
structure.

5.4   *IS stock amendments program*
An indexed sequential version of the stock
master file specified in Exercise 4.4 is to be
updated and amended by random
processing, with transactions contained in a
serial validated stock amendments file.
There are five types of record within the
stock amendments file, identified by a
record type code contained in the same
position within each record and having the
following possible values.

Code

A   a new record to be added to file

D   a record to be deleted from file

C   the reorder level (indicated by change
type code 1) or price (indicated by
change type code 2) in a record has to
be changed

I   issue record

R   receipt record } as for Exercise 5.3

It is possible that an amendment record (of
types D, C, I and R) has no matching master
record. Furthermore it is possible that an
amendment record of type A does have a
matching master record. Such errors should
be identified by displaying the error
amendment records in an unpaged error
report without report headings.

For this program you are required to:

(a)   Produce data structures for all files;

(b)   Identify correspondences;

(c)   Produce matched data structures;

(d)   Produce a preliminary program
structure.

6 Producing the detailed design

With the production of the individual data structures associated with a program, and their matching to produce a preliminary program structure, the most difficult stages in JSP have been accomplished. The remaining stages, which lead to the detailed program design, are more mechanical and are addressed in this chapter.

What has been achieved with the production of a preliminary program structure is an identification of the major parts (i.e. components) of the program, and in particular the function of each component and the relationship of each with the others. This chapter will concentrate on the next three steps of the JSP method, which identify the conditions that control the iteration and selection relationships, refine certain of the components into detailed actions and lastly produce the final version of the program structure.

The first section of this chapter will discuss the identification and allocation of conditions. The second, third and fourth sections will look at the problem of identifying actions and the allocation of these actions to relevant components of the program structure. As a result of allocating actions to the preliminary version of the program structure, the latter may become invalid in relation to the second fundamental principle of structured program design discussed in Chapter 2. The final section of this chapter will discuss this particular problem and how it may be resolved by revising the program structure. The primary example used for illustrative purposes in this chapter will be the merge program of Example 5.2.

Identifying and allocating conditions

Non-elementary components (i.e. sequences, selections and iterations) within a program structure are sometimes referred to as 'control' components because their function is to control when their child components are executed in the final program. In particular selection and iteration components control whether their child components are executed or not through specific conditions. To help clarify this it will help to appreciate the impact of these two component types on the eventual detailed program design and hence the eventual source program. In Chapter 2 you were introduced to a program description language which may be used to describe the detailed program design prior to translation into source code. This program description language is used in Figure 6.1 to show the impact of iterations and selections on the eventual detailed design. What has been illustrated is that for every iteration and for every selected component of a selection a condition must be identified which will cause that iteration or selection to be executed.

The first phase in this process is to identify all conditions which may arise during execution of the program by again examining the program specification in detail. In Chapter 3 you were advised that the correct data structures could only be achieved by a good understanding of the processing requirements of the program. It was suggested that simulating the detailed processing of the program using some simple data would greatly enhance your understanding of the required program. It is advised that you repeat the simulation in order to help you identify the conditions which will arise during processing. The conditions identified should be documented as a list in any order.

Guidelines for condition identification
The following guidelines should help you to produce a list of conditions:

1 *Examine the program specification*, not the program structure, as explained in the previous paragraph.
2 *Number the conditions* but make no attempt to place them in any order. Use the numbering convention C1, C2, C3 etc., the C being used

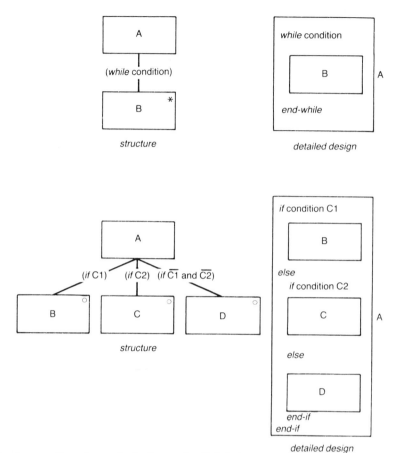

Figure 6.1   *Impact of iterations and selections on detailed design*

to clearly differentiate between conditions and actions. The numbers will be used to document the allocation of the conditions to the program structure.

3   *Where possible, avoid source programming language*   Conditions should be written in unambiguous English and should be expressed as questions.

4   *Identify 'simple' conditions* only, i.e. not involving 'and' or 'or'. Compound conditions should be broken down into a set of simple conditions.

5   *Avoid negative conditions*, e.g. not end of file.

6   *Look for conditions associated with processing data*, i.e. files, record groups, records and items. Common examples of conditions arising are:

End of input sequential file?
End of record group?
End of report page?
Record present in an indexed sequential master file?
Master record key = transaction record key?
Master record key < transaction record key?
Master record key > transaction record key?
Record type = X?
Item X < item Y?

C1   End of first input file?

C2   End of second input file?

C3   First input record key = second input record key?

C4   First input record key < second input record key?

C5   First input record key > second input record key?

Figure 6.2   *Conditions list for merge program*

Using these guidelines, the resulting conditions list for the merge program of Example 5.2 would be as documented in Figure 6.2. One point arising from this list is that condition C5 is actually unnecessary because C5 = $\overline{C3}$ AND $\overline{C4}$, where the bar over a condition indicates the negation of that condition. Hence condition C5 could be omitted from the list.

Guidelines for condition allocation

The next phase of the process is to allocate each of the conditions to iterations and/or selections within the preliminary program structure. The following guidelines should help you in this process:

1   *Work top-down through the structure, considering each iteration and selection in turn*   Consider each iteration and selection in turn by working through the levels of the program structure from the highest (i.e. the root component) to the lowest.

2   *For an iteration construct* ask the following question:

In order to process the 'father component' the program needs to keep processing the 'child component' *while what condition is true?*

The condition that may eventually be chosen could be a simple condition, the negative of a simple condition, or a compound condition containing two or more simple conditions from the conditions list. Incidentally you should clarify the rules for forming compound conditions before proceeding any further; in particular you should ensure that you understand De Morgan's law, which can be used to simplify compound conditions.

3   *For a selection construct* ask the following question for each selected child component:

In order to process the 'father component' the program needs to process the 'child component' *if what condition is true?*

4   *A condition may be allocated to one or more iterations and/or selected components*   However, if at the end of this process a condition has not been allocated, then review the condition and if necessary review the preliminary program structure and its related data structures.

5   *Concatenation of conditions*   Simple conditions associated with iterations may concatenate down the program structure and be a part of the conditions associated with lower-level iterations and selections.

6   *Exhaustive coverage of all possible conditions*   You should ensure that all the conditions associated with an iteration or a selection exhaustively cover all possible conditions that may arise on entry to that component. In particular, within a selection, *all* conditions which will lead to a particular component being selected should be explicitly identified.

7   *Do not use ELSE within a selection*   This guideline is closely associated with the last. Sometimes it is tempting not to explicitly assign a condition to the rightmost branch of a selection component but simply to define the branch as ELSE, e.g. as shown in Figure 6.3. The intention is to specify that under all other conditions associated with the selection, i.e. other than those which lead to the other branches of the selection being selected, that branch should be selected. However, there are two reasons why this practice should be

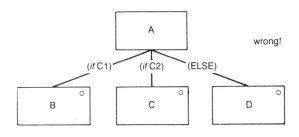

Figure 6.3   *Solution with ELSE*

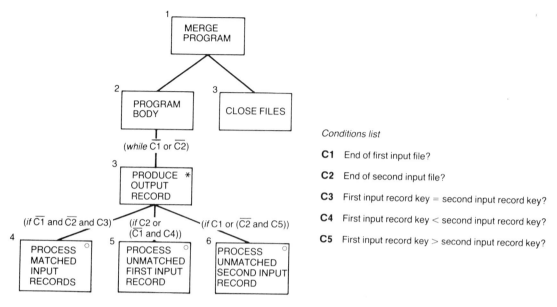

Figure 6.4   *Program structure with allocated conditions for merge program*

discouraged. First, it could lead to failure to identify certain conditions which could arise. Second, it presupposes the order in which the conditions will be tested and the selected components will be implemented. It is not the intention in JSP that the order of the selected components in a selection construct has any significance; the selected components could be implemented in any order.

If these guidelines are used for the merge program whose preliminary program structure was given in Figure 5.11, the allocation of conditions would be as in Figure 6.4. In this example you should note in particular the conditions associated with the selection; these conditions account for all possible situations, including the end-of-file record of one input file being processed with a data record from the other input file.

Identifying actions

The program structure diagram produced after the second step of the JSP method represents the 'skeleton' of the program. The relation between this skeleton structure and the final source program can be illustrated by translating the program structure of Figure 6.4 into the program description language. The result is as in Figure 6.5.

What Figure 6.5 illustrates is that the 'flesh' to be added to the skeleton structure is the detailed

actions necessary to implement the functions to be performed by the elementary components in the program structure. In Figure 6.5 these elementary components are PROCESS MATCHED INPUT RECORDS, PROCESS UNMATCHED FIRST INPUT RECORD, PROCESSED UNMATCHED SECOND INPUT RECORD and CLOSE FILES. As for conditions, this is a two-stage process requiring the identification of the detailed actions and then

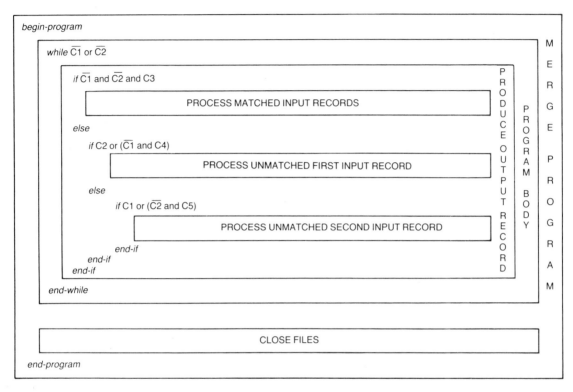

Figure 6.5   *Program structure for merge program represented in program description language*

the allocation of these actions to the components of the program structure. The first of these stages is to be explained in this section and the second stage in the following section.

The first stage is then to identify all the actions which could arise in the execution of the program and document them as a numbered list. The following guidelines should help you to produce a complete list of actions:

1   *Examine the program specification, not the preliminary program structure*   The detailed actions should be relinquished by examining the program specification, not the program structure, because this procedure will help to validate the preliminary program structure in the allocation stage. In order to extract the actions from the program specification, the same advice that was given earlier is repeated: simulate the detailed processing, and hence identify the detailed actions that are required

of the program, using simple data.

2   *Number the actions but make no attempt to place them in order of operation*   As you identify actions add them to a numbered list but make no attempt to place them in any order. The reason for numbering them is to avoid cluttering the program structure during the allocation stage.

3   *Where possible, avoid source programming language*   The actions should be written in English, and be imperative and unambiguous. The level of detail should, however, be approximately that of the level of source programming language statements.

4   *The majority of actions will arise out of operations on data*   It may help you to bear in mind that the majority of actions will arise out of operations on the various levels of data, i.e. files, record groups, records and items. For instance, actions may be required for any or all

of the following:

(a)   Open and close files.
(b)   Read record from file.
(c)   Set up output record.
(d)   Output record to file.
(e)   Initialize totals, counters and table subscripts.
(f)   Calculate totals, and increment counters and pointers.
(g)   Actions required to implement conditions, e.g. save key of record before reading next record, in order to check for change in key.

However, other actions may not directly be concerned with operations on data, for instance:

(h)   Stop execution of the program.

5   *Avoid non-imperative actions*   'Actions' of the type TEST FOR END OF FILE or COMPARE A WITH B are in fact conditions, not actions, and should appear in the conditions list.

1	Stop program.
2	Open first input file.
3	Open second input file.
4	Open merged output file.
5	Close first input file.
6	Close second input file.
7	Close merged output file.
8	Read record from first input file.
9	Read record from second input file.
10	Copy first input record to merged output record area.
11	Copy second input record to merged output record area.
12	Output record to merged output file.

Figure 6.6   *Actions list for merge program*

6   *Avoid omnibus actions* such as ZEROIZE ALL TOTALS or OPEN ALL FILES because these can lead to confusion during the allocation stage.

If these guidelines are applied to the merge program of Example 5.2, the list of actions in Figure 6.6 is identified.

Allocation of actions

The next stage is to allocate each of the actions to one or more of the components in the preliminary program structure and therefore eventually to identify the actions necessary to implement the function of each elementary component. The actions should be examined in the order in which they occur in the actions list. For each action the following procedure should be applied:

1   *Identify the component or components to which the action should be allocated* by asking the following two questions:

(a)   *Upon what data is the action operating*, i.e. to what data component or components is this action applicable?
   Is it a file? Which file?
   Is it a record group? Which record group?
   Is it a record ? Which record?

It is an item? Which item?
The answer could be no component, or one or more components. In the latter cases it is likely that the action will be allocated to the program component(s) corresponding with the identified data component(s).

(b)   *How often should this action be done?*
   Once for the program or file?
   Once per record group?
   Once per record?
   Once per type X record?
   etc.
A similar question needs to be asked about each program component.

As a result of the answers to these two questions it should be possible to identify the program component(s) to which the action

should be allocated. In some cases actions may
have been identified with non-elementary
components. This situation can arise and will
be resolved by minor modifications to the
program structure in the next step of the JSP
method described later in this chapter. For the
time being you can allocate actions to non-
elementary components, but if ever there is a
choice you should avoid it.

2 *If the action is a read action* associated with a
   serial/sequential file it may require special
   treatment. This is covered in the next section.

3 *Unallocated actions*   If no appropriate
   component can be found for an action, then
   either the action's meaning is not clear, or you
   should review the need for the action, or you
   should review the program structure.

4 *Allocate the action to the identified component(s)
   on the program structure diagram*   It is now
   possible to write the action number, from the
   actions list, under its corresponding box(es)
   on the program structure design, for example
   as shown in Figure 6.7.

   However, if the component is a non-
elementary component and/or already has
actions allocated, the following question needs
to be asked:

Should the action to be allocated be done
before or after each of the already allocated
actions and/or in the case of a non-elementary
component, component(s)?

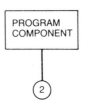

Figure 6.7   *Allocation of action to a program component*

Figure 6.8 (overleaf) shows the result of applying
the steps of the above procedure to the merge
program of Example 5.2, using the data structure
diagrams of Figure 5.10, the program structure
diagram of Figure 6.4 and the actions list of
Figure 6.6. The allocation of the read actions has
been left until the special problems associated
with them are discussed in the next section.

   It is possible after the allocation of actions to a
program structure that an elementary program
component may not have actions allocated to it. If
this does arise it could be that there are
unidentified actions or that an error has occurred
in the production of the program structure.
Alternatively, in very exceptional circumstances it
may be because the component is legitimately an
'empty' component, i.e. a component requiring
no actions to be executed.

(a)

	Action	Applicable data component(s)	Corresponding program component(s)
1	Stop program	None	?
2	Open first input file	FIRST INPUT FILE	MERGE PROGRAM
3	Open second input file	SECOND INPUT FILE	MERGE PROGRAM
4	Open merged output file	MERGED OUTPUT FILE	MERGE PROGRAM
5	Close first input file	END-OF-FILE RECORD	CLOSE FILES
6	Close second input file	END-OF-FILE RECORD	CLOSE FILES
7	Close merged output file	END-OF-FILE-RECORD	CLOSE FILES
8	Read record from first input file	MATCHED FIRST INPUT RECORD UNMATCHED FIRST INPUT RECORD	PROCESS MATCHED INPUT RECORDS PROCESS UNMATCHED FIRST INPUT RECORD
9	Read record from second input file	MATCHED SECOND INPUT RECORD UNMATCHED SECOND INPUT RECORD	PROCESS MATCHED INPUT RECORDS PROCESS UNMATCHED SECOND INPUT RECORD
10	Copy first input record to merged output record area	MATCHED FIRST INPUT RECORD UNMATCHED FIRST INPUT RECORD	PROCESS MATCHED INPUT RECORDS PROCESS UNMATCHED FIRST INPUT RECORD
11	Copy second input record to merged output record area	UNMATCHED SECOND INPUT RECORD	PROCESS UNMATCHED SECOND INPUT RECORD
12	Output record to merged output file	MATCHED FIRST INPUT RECORD UNMATCHED FIRST INPUT RECORD UNMATCHED SECOND INPUT RECORD	PROCESS MATCHED INPUT RECORDS PROCESS UNMATCHED FIRST INPUT RECORD PROCESS UNMATCHED SECOND INPUT RECORD

(b)

Action	Number of times done	Program component(s) to which action is allocated
1	Once per program	MERGE PROGRAM
2	Once per program	MERGE PROGRAM
3	Once per program	MERGE PROGRAM
4	Once per program	MERGE PROGRAM
5	Once per end-of-file record	CLOSE FILES
6	Once per end-of-file record	CLOSE FILES
7	Once per end-of-file record	CLOSE FILES
8	Once per record in first input file plus once for end-of-file record	?
9	Once per record in second input file plus once for end-of-file record	?
10	Once per matched first input record plus once per unmatched first input record	PROCESS MATCHED INPUT RECORDS PROCESS UNMATCHED FIRST INPUT RECORD
11	Once per unmatched second input record	PROCESS UNMATCHED SECOND INPUT RECORD
12	Once per matched first input record plus once per unmatched first input record plus once per unmatched second input record	PROCESS MATCHED INPUT RECORDS PROCESS UNMATCHED FIRST INPUT RECORD PROCESS UNMATCHED SECOND INPUT RECORD

(c)

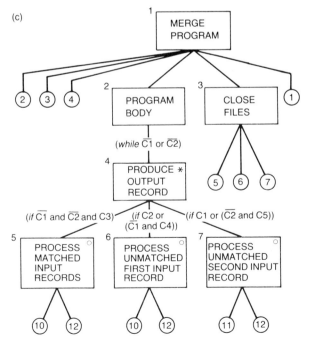

Conditions list

C1 End of first input file?

C2 End of second input file?

C3 First input record key = second input record key?

C4 First input record key < second input record key?

C5 First input record key > second input record key?

Figure 6.8 (a) Result after step 1(a); (b) Result after steps 1, 2, 3; (c) Result after step 4 with read actions unallocated

Read actions and read ahead

When allocating actions to a program structure, read actions associated with a serial/sequential input file may require special treatment.

Consider the program structure, with allocated actions, depicted in Figure 6.9, for a program which processes a file consisting of exactly three records. In practice the actions 1, 2 and 3 in particular are too ill defined, but in this circumstance they will suffice. With this example the allocation of the read action is correct because it is known that each record will be present, in the correct order, within the file.

However, now consider the program structure in Figure 6.8(c). This structure clearly requires the *first* record in each of the two input files to be available for inspection on entry to the iteration component PROGRAM BODY and on first entry to the selection component PRODUCE OUTPUT RECORD, in order that conditions C1 and C2 can be evaluated. A similar argument applies to the *next* record for each file. Also, Figure 6.8(b) clearly states that the read actions 8 and 9 must be done one more time than there are records in their respective files.

A procedure known as 'read ahead' must be used to overcome these two problems. This requires that for most programs processing an input serial/sequential file:

1 A read action (read *first*) should be placed at the start of the program, following the respective 'open file' action.
2 A read action (read *next*) should be allocated to the component(s) where a record is completely processed, normally as the last action in that component.

The effect of reading ahead is that:

1 Outside any component which processes a record, the record area contains the next record to be processed.
2 On entry to a component which processes a record, the record which was next becomes the current record.
3 On exit from a component which processes a record, the current record is replaced by the next.

The impact of allocating the read actions to the program structure of Figure 6.8(c) using the read ahead principle is shown in Figure 6.10. Some users of JSP would split the read action into two explicit actions, 'read first' and 'read next', claiming that this practice leads to greater clarity.

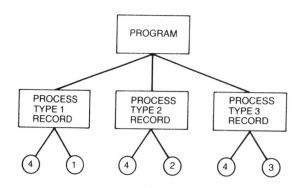

Action list

1 Process type 1 record.
2 Process type 2 record.
3 Process type 3 record.
4 Read a record.

Figure 6.9   *Example not requiring read ahead*

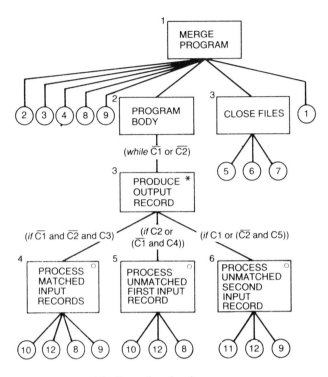

Figure 6.10 *Merge program structure with allocated read actions*

Producing final program structure

The second fundamental principle of JSP is that the program structure should consist of only sequence, selection, iteration and elementary components. Sequence, selection and iteration components should perform only control functions, i.e. they only control the execution of their child component(s). An elementary component, on the other hand, performs a detailed function of the program which can be expressed as one or more imperative actions. What this means is that the final program structure should only have actions allocated to elementary components.

As a result of steps 2, 3 and 4 of the JSP method it is likely that a program structure will be derived with some actions allocated to non-elementary components. This is certainly true for the merge program whose preliminary program structure with allocated actions is shown in Figure 6.10. In this particular example six actions have been allocated to the sequence component MERGE PROGRAM.

The main reason for this invalidity arising at this stage in the execution of the JSP method is that the preliminary program structure was derived from the structure of the data to be processed by the program. If you remember, the reason that the JSP method takes this approach is because of the third fundamental principle of JSP, discussed in Chapter 2, which is that the processing carried out by data processing programs is dictated by the characteristics of the data being processed. However, although this is true, not all the actions arising in a program will necessarily directly arise out of processing the data components identified in the data structures; an obvious example is that of the action 'stop program'. As a result certain actions are allocated to non-elementary components in the preliminary program structure, and hence the program structure does not represent a truly structured program design.

This invalidity may easily be removed by applying the following procedure:

1   *If one or more actions have been allocated to a sequence component*: add a further child component with a relevant name to the sequence to which the action(s) are allocated and/or allocate the action(s) to an existing elementary child component whose name should be revised to reflect its more generalized function. Hence the program

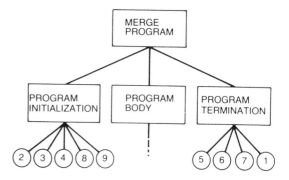

Figure 6.11   *Revised MERGE PROGRAM component*

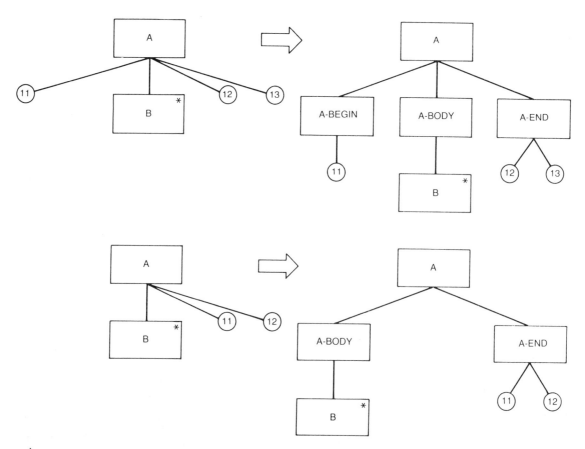

Figure 6.12   *Mechanisms for converting invalid iteration construct into a valid structure*

structure in Figure 6.10 could be made valid by making the changes illustrated in Figure 6.11.

2   *If one or more actions have been allocated to an iteration component*: introduce an extra level to the program structure, between the iteration component and its child component, consisting of two or three (whichever is applicable) sequenced components with relevant names as illustrated in Figure 6.12.

3   *If one or more actions have been allocated to a selection component*: introduce an extra level to the program structure, between the selection component and its child components, consisting of two or three (whichever is applicable) sequenced components with relevant names. This is the same procedure as described for iteration components in 2.

As a result of applying this procedure the final version of the program structure is produced; for the merge program this is as in Figure 6.13.

Another possible change that may be required to a program structure diagram arises from the possibility of an elementary program component(s) with no allocated actions, i.e. an 'empty' component. If the component is a sequenced component then it may be safely removed from the program structure. This may lead to the respective parent sequence component having only one child component, in which case the remaining child component may also be removed, as illustrated in Figure 6.14.

If the empty component is a selected component, then the empty component should be retained so that all alternatives to a selection are explicitly included. It is impossible for an iterated component to be empty unless an error has occurred in the production of the program structure.

A further possible change may be required to sequence components when the sequenced components arise from data components representing data items. It was explained in Chapter 3 that the data items of a record may be accessed in any order and as many times as required by a program. Hence sequenced components arising from data items may be

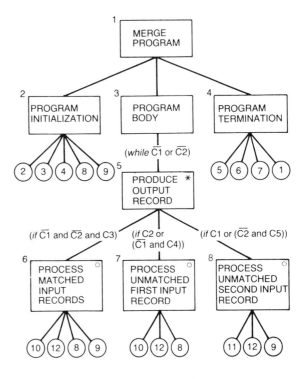

Figure 6.13   *Valid program structure for merge program*

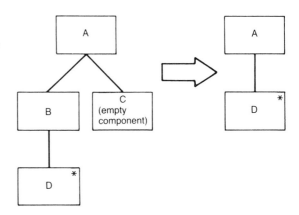

Figure 6.14   *Revision to program structure arising from empty component*

reordered for the convenience of processing. Furthermore, additional sequenced components may be required because certain data items are processed more than once.

Exercises

Produce:

(a)   The conditions list
(b)   The actions list
(c)   The final program structure with allocated actions and conditions

for each of the following programs. A preliminary program structure for each of these programs is given in the 'Solutions to exercises'.

6.1   *Employees holidays program*
The program is specified in Exercise 4.2.
6.2   *Job costing program (second version)*
The program is specified in Exercise 4.3.
6.3   *Update stock master program (second version)*
The program is specified in Exercise 5.3.
6.4   *IS stock amendments program*
The program is specified in Exercise 5.4.

7 Beyond design – coding

With the production of the final version of the program structure with allocated actions and conditions, the last step of the JSP design method is completed. The next stage of the program development process is to convert this design into code. This can be done manually or semi-automatically, using one of the available software packages, called preprocessors, designed for this purpose. If it is done manually there are three basic ways of doing it and within these there are many variations, some depending on the programming language being used. Jackson advocates that if it is done manually, the program design is converted into a program description language (similar to the one introduced in Chapter 2) called 'schematic logic' as an intermediate stage between the design and the source code. However, the use of a program description language, in particular schematic logic, can be applied only when using two out of the three basic conversion methods.

A potential problem that may arise in converting a JSP design into code is in the implementation of reading ahead. This may be difficult or impossible in some programming languages, e.g. Pascal, where a predetermined format is required for each read statement, i.e. the precise format of the record must be known on reading. This causes problems when the input file consists of records of more than one type, i.e. format.

It is not the intention in this chapter to discuss the facilities of any programming language or preprocessor software in detail. Nor is it the intention to discuss in detail any method of converting a design into code. The first section of this chapter will introduce Jackson's schematic logic. The second, third and fourth sections will describe the three basic ways of manually converting a JSP design into code using the programming languages BASIC, Pascal and COBOL for illustrative purposes. The fifth section will give an overview of two of the preprocessor software packages available, which automate the conversion of design into code.

Schematic logic

Schematic logic (or 'structure text') is a program description language similar to the one described in Chapter 2. The use of schematic logic has the following advantages:

1   It can provide a valuable bridge between the program design and the source code.
2   It is used as input to various 'schematic logic preprocessors' which are available on the market. Schematic logic preprocessors are discussed later in the chapter.
3   Particular classes of problem addressed by JSP, which are discussed in Chapters 8 and 9, have solutions in which schematic logic plays an important role.

Schematic logic is best explained through an example. The example chosen is the schematic logic equivalent to the program design for the merge program given in Figure 6.13.

The schematic logic for this example is given in Figure 7.1 (overleaf).

The rules which are applied to convert a program structure, with allocated actions and conditions, into schematic logic are:

1   *The various levels of the program structure* are emphasized by using indentation. The vertical lines in Figure 7.1 indicate each level of the program structure from the highest (zeroth) to lowest (third), represented from left to right.
2   *The limits of a sequence component* are indicated by the delimiters:

component-name *seq*

.

.

.

component-name *end*

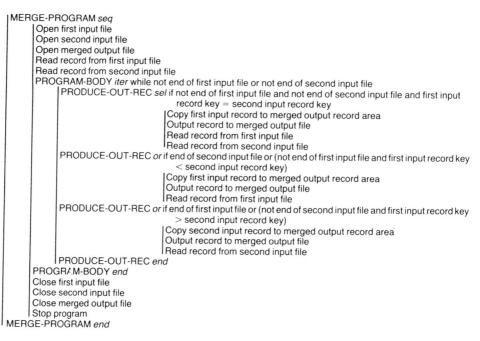

Figure 7.1   *Schematic logic representation of design for merge program*

where 'component-name' is either the
component name used in the program
structure diagram, or a shortened but still
recognizable form of it, or the component
number used in the program structure
diagram.

3   *The limits of an iteration component* are
indicated by the delimiters:

component-name *iter* while 'condition'

.

.

.

component-name *end*

where 'condition' is the condition allocated to
the iteration on the program structure
diagram.

4   *The limits of a selection component* are indicated
as follows:

component-name *sel* if 'condition-1'

.

.

.

component-name *or* if 'condition-2' ⎫ may be
⎪ repeated
⎬ if further
. ⎪ selected
. ⎭ components

.

.

component-name *end*

where condition-1, condition-2, etc. are the
conditions allocated to each branch of the
selection on the program structure diagram.

5   *An elementary component* is not explicitly
identified but is represented by the list of
actions allocated to that component on the
program structure diagram.

The use of schematic logic is not applicable, and
therefore not recommended, if the intention is to
convert the program design into 'hierarchic code'
which is described in the next section.

Conversion to hierarchic code

Converting the program design into hierarchic code means that each component, other than the root, in the program structure diagram is represented by a subroutine. The facilities within programming languages for implementing subroutines vary immensely. In standard BASIC the only facility available is called a subroutine. In COBOL two facilities are available, namely the internal subroutine (sections and/or paragraphs) and the subprogram (or external subroutine). In Pascal the facility is called the procedure. No attempt is made within this text to explain these various facilities or to discuss in detail the implementation of hierarchic code in any of the three programming languages. Instead an implementation, using hierarchic code, of the program design for a simple program is given in each of the three languages.

Example 7.1 *Sign count program*
The input to a program consists of a series of

non-zero integer numbers, each of which may be positive or negative. The series of numbers is terminated by a zero number. The program is required to count the total number of positive and the total number of negative numbers in the input, and output values of the two counts. The program design for this example is as in Figure 7.2.

A representation of this program design in hierarchic code using each of the three languages BASIC, Pascal and COBOL (using paragraphs) is given in Figure 7.3. The detailed code presented in these examples is not intended to represent good coding practice or indeed the only solution; it is presented for the sole purpose of illustrating the way hierarchic code may be implemented in the three languages. A number of points arise from these three example sections of code.

The first is a general one concerning the implementation of a selection component. The branches of a selection component can be

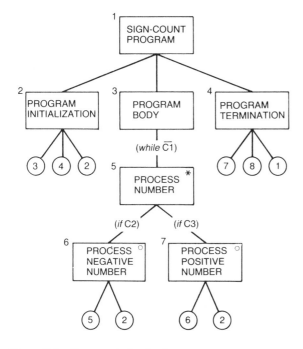

Conditions list

C1 Number $= 0$
C2 Number < 0
C3 Number > 0

Actions list

1 Stop program.
2 Read number.
3 Zeroize negative count.
4 Zeroize positive count.
5 Increase negative count by 1.
6 Increase positive count by 1.
7 Print negative count.
8 Print positive count.

Figure 7.2 *Program design for sign count program*

(a)

```
100   REM*SIGN-COUNT PROGRAM
110   GOSUB 200
120   GOSUB 300
130   GOSUB 400

200   REM*PROGRAM INITIALIZATION
210   LET C1 = 0
220   LET C2 = 0
230   INPUT N
240   RETURN

300   REM*PROGRAM BODY
310   IF N = 0 THEN 340
320   GOSUB 500
330   GOTO 310
340   RETURN

400   REM*PROGRAM TERMINATION
410   PRINT "NEGATIVE COUNT = ";C1
420   PRINT "POSITIVE COUNT = ";C2
430   STOP
440   RETURN

500   REM*PROCESS NUMBER
510   IF N > 0 THEN 540
520   GOSUB 600
530   GOTO 550
540   GOSUB 700
550   RETURN

600   REM*PROCESS NEGATIVE NUMBER
610   LET C1 = C1 + 1
620   INPUT N
630   RETURN

700   REM*PROCESS POSITIVE NUMBER
710   LET C2 = C2 + 1
720   INPUT N
730   RETURN

740   END
```

(b)

```
program signcount (input, output);

var number, negativecount, positivecount : integer;

procedure processnegativenumber;
begin
        negativecount := negativecount + 1;
        read (number)
end;

procedure processpositivenumber;
begin
        positivecount := positivecount + 1;
        read (number)
end;

procedure processnumber;
begin
    if number < 0 then
            processnegativenumber
    else
            processpositivenumber
end;

procedure programinitialization;
begin
        negativecount := 0;
        positivecount := 0;
        read (number)
end;

procedure programbody;
begin
    while number <> 0 do
            processnumber
end;

procedure programtermination;
begin
        writeln ('negative count = ',negativecount);
        writeln ('positive count = ',positivecount)
end;

begin;
        programinitialization;
        programbody;
        programtermination
end.
```

Figure 7.3   (a) Hierarchic code in BASIC; (b) Hierarchic code in Pascal; (c) Hierarchic code in COBOL

implemented in any order. However, unless there is a good reason (e.g. optimization; see Chapter 12) it is best to implement them in the order depicted in the program structure, i.e. from left to right.

The second is also a general one concerning the implementation of the last branch of a selection component. The last branch of a selection component should be selected if the conditions associated with all the other branches are false. If this is not true then there is a potential error in the program. Hence in implementing the last branch of a selection it should be unnecessary to test for

any condition. This is reflected in the examples of Figure 7.3, in particular in the Pascal and COBOL examples, where ELSE has been used.

The third point concerns the order in which the subroutines (i.e. the implemented components) are presented in the code. They should be presented in such an order that the relationship between the program design and code is simple and clear. The components have been implemented and coded level by level. For COBOL and BASIC this means in top-down order. However for Pascal, because of restrictions in the language, they are presented in bottom-up

(c)
```
 PROCEDURE DIVISION.

 SIGN-COUNT-PROGRAM.
     PERFORM PROGRAM-INITIALIZATION.
     PERFORM PROGRAM-BODY.
     PERFORM PROGRAM-TERMINATION.

 PROGRAM-INITIALIZATION.
     MOVE ZERO TO NEGATIVE-COUNT.
     MOVE ZERO TO POSITIVE-COUNT.
     ACCEPT NUMBER.

 PROGRAM-BODY.
     PERFORM PROCESS-NUMBER UNTIL NUMBER = 0.

 PROGRAM-TERMINATION.
     DISPLAY "NEGATIVE COUNT = ", NEGATIVE-COUNT.
     DISPLAY "POSITIVE COUNT = ", POSITIVE-COUNT.
     STOP RUN.

 PROCESS-NUMBER.
     IF NUMBER IS LESS THAN ZERO
                     PERFORM PROCESS-NEGATIVE-NUMBER
         ELSE
                     PERFORM PROCESS-POSITIVE-NUMBER.

 PROCESS-NEGATIVE-NUMBER.
     ADD 1 TO NEGATIVE-COUNT.
     ACCEPT NUMBER.

 PROCESS-POSITIVE-NUMBER.
     ADD 1 TO POSITIVE-COUNT.
     ACCEPT NUMBER.
```

order, i.e. starting at the lowest level. However, an alternative to level-by-level order, whether top-down or bottom-up, is to implement the program branch by branch working from left to right. For COBOL and BASIC this means the component number order of 1, 2, 3, 5, 6, 7, 4. However, this method could not be applied in Pascal.

The fourth point concerns the advantages and disadvantages of using hierarchic code. Hierarchic code is not recommended for languages where subroutines cannot be named (e.g. in standard BASIC) because it leads to a loss of clarity in the relationship between code and design. Furthermore it is not recommended for languages where subroutines require complicated syntax (e.g. in Pascal procedures for parameter passing) because of the increased problem of syntax errors. However, hierarchic code for COBOL, if paragraphs are used, is easy to write and there is a clear and simple relationship between code and design.

However, hierarchic code in general can waste both coding time and run time, because of the coding and run-time overheads of subroutine calls. Furthermore some JSP techniques, such as inversion and backtracking (discussed in Chapters 8 and 9), are not compatible with hierarchic code.

Conversion to nested code

Schematic logic, described at the beginning of the chapter, is based on language features introduced in the programming language ALGOL in the early 1960s and now available in the programming languages Pascal and PL/1 and to a lesser extent in FORTRAN 77 and some implementations of BASIC. In these languages there are facilities enabling a source program to be produced which resembles very closely the schematic logic equivalent. The code produced is referred to as 'nested code', or sometimes 'structured code', because the code representing the child component(s) is included (or nested) within the code representing the parent component. Nested code is best illustrated with an example. Figure

```
SIGN-COUNT seq
  | Zeroize negative count
  | Zeroize positive count
  | Read number
  | PROGRAM-BODY iter while number not = 0
  |   | PROCESS-NUMBER sel if number < 0
  |   |   | Increase negative count by 1
  |   |   | Read number
  |   | PROCESS-NUMBER or if number > 0
  |   |   | Increase positive count by 1
  |   |   | Read number
  |   | PROCESS-NUMBER end
  | PROGRAM-BODY end
  | Print negative count
  | Print positive count
  | Stop program
SIGN-COUNT end
```

Figure 7.4 *Schematic logic for sign count program*

(a)
```
program signcount (input, output);
var number, negativecount, positivecount : integer;

begin
(*sign-count :seq*)
        negativecount := 0;
        positivecount := 0;
        read(number);
        (*program-body:iter*)
        while number <> 0 do
        begin
                (*process-number:sel*)
                if number < 0 then
                        begin
                                negativecount := negativecount + 1;
                                read (number)
                        end
                (*process-number:or*)
                else
                        begin
                                positivecount := positivecount + 1;
                                read (number)
                        end;
                (*process-number:end*)
        end
        (*program-body-end*)
        writeln ('negative count =',negativecount);
        writeln ('positive count = ', positivecount);
(*sign-count:end*)
end.
```

(b)
```
100   REM*SIGN-COUNT PROGRAM:SEQ
110     LET C1=0
120     LET C2=0
130     INPUT N
140     REM*PROGRAM BODY :ITER
150     WHILE N <> 0
160       REM*PROCESS NUMBER : SEL
170       IF N < 0 THEN DO
180         LET C1=C1+1
190         INPUT N
200       REM*PROCESS NUMBER : OR
210       ELSE
220         LET C2=C2+1
230         INPUT N
240       DOEND
250       REM*PROCESS NUMBER : END
260     ELIHW
270     REM*PROGRAM BODY : END
280     PRINT "NEGATIVE COUNT ="; C1
290     PRINT "POSITIVE COUNT ="; C2
300     STOP
310   REM*SIGN-COUNT PROGRAM : END
320   END
```

Figure 7.5   *(a) Nested code in Pascal; (b) Nested code in a structured BASIC*

7.4 contains the schematic logic representation of the program design depicted in Figure 7.2. Figure 7.5 contains nested code equivalents of this schematic logic in Pascal and a non-standard implementation of BASIC (referred to as structured BASIC). An example of nested code in COBOL is not given because COBOL 74 does not have the facilities for its implementation. However it is extremely likely that the new COBOL standard,[3] to be published shortly, will have such facilities. It can be seen in Figure 7.5 that the code produced, aided by indentation and comments, demonstrates a close relationship between the code and the schematic logic equivalent.

Another characteristic of the code is the notable absence of 'goto' statements. However, 'goto' statements would be required to implement the JSP technique of 'backtracking'.

Conversion to flat code

This form of code avoids subroutines and nesting. It uses conditions, labels and GOTOs to express the structure. It is really an alternative to nested code for those languages, such as COBOL 74 and standard BASIC, which do not have the language facilities to implement nested code. The ideal method to produce flat code is to convert the schematic logic line by line, converting:

1   A component beginning or end into a paragraph name in COBOL or a REM statement in BASIC;

2   An iteration construct according to the
     following examples:

Schematic logic	COBOL	BASIC
	XYZ-ITER.	200 REM*XYZ-ITER
XYZ *iter* while C1	IF NOT	210 IF NOT (C1) THEN 310
	(C1) GO TO XYZ-END.	
.		.
.	.	.
.		.
XYZ *end*	GO TO XYZ-ITER.	300 GOTO 200
	XYZ-END.	310 REM*XYZ-END

3   A selection construct according to the
     following examples:

Schematic logic	COBOL	BASIC
	XYZ-SEL.	200 REM*XYZ-SEL
XYZ *sel* if C1	IF NOT	210 IF NOT (C1) THEN 300
	(C1) GO TO XYZ-OR1.	
.		.
.	.	.
.		.
XYZ *or* if C2	GO TO XYZ-END.	290 GOTO 500
.	XYZ-OR1.	300 REM*XYZ-OR1
.	IF NOT	310 IF NOT (C2) THEN 400
.	(C) GO TO XYZ-OR2.	.
.		
.	.	.
XYZ *or* if C3	.	.
.		.
.	GO TO XYZ-END.	390 GOTO 500
	XYZ-OR2.	400 REM*XYZ-OR2
XYZ *end*		
	.	.
	.	.
	XYZ-END.	500 REM*XYZ-END

4   An action into its programming language
     equivalent.

Figure 7.6 contains the flat code equivalents in
COBOL and BASIC for the schematic logic
depicted in Figure 7.4.

A particularly significant aspect of flat code
representation is the use of the GOTO statement
required to implement iterations and selections.
Structured programming purists advocate the
non-use of the GOTO statement, claiming that its
use can lead to programs which are difficult to
read and understand. However, the author would
advocate that in the flat code implementation of a
JSP design the GOTO is used in a controlled way
that does not lead to major difficulties of
readability and understandability. Furthermore
the use of the GOTO statement is unavoidable
with the facilities available at present in the
common programming languages when
implementing the JSP features of backtracking
and inversion, which are discussed in Chapters 8
and 9.

(a)
```
PROCEDURE DIVISION.
SIGN-COUNT-SEQ.
      MOVE ZERO TO NEGATIVE-COUNT.
      MOVE ZERO TO POSITIVE-COUNT.
      ACCEPT NUMBER.
PROGRAM-BODY-ITER.
      IF NUMBER = 0 GO TO PROGRAM-BODY-END.
PROCESS-NUMBER-SEL.
      IF NUMBER > 0 GO TO PROCESS-NUMBER-OR.
      ADD 1 TO NEGATIVE-COUNT.
      ACCEPT NUMBER.
      GO TO PROCESS-NUMBER-END.
PROCESS-NUMBER-OR.
      ADD 1 TO POSITIVE-COUNT.
      ACCEPT NUMBER.
PROCESS-NUMBER-END.
      GO TO PROGRAM-BODY-ITER.
PROGRAM-BODY-END.
      DISPLAY "NEGATIVE COUNT =", NEGATIVE-COUNT.
      DISPLAY "POSITIVE COUNT=", POSITIVE-COUNT.
      STOP PROGRAM.
SIGN-COUNT-END.
```

(b)
```
100   REM*SIGN-COUNT-SEQ
110   LET C1=0
120   LET C2=0
130   INPUT N
140   REM*PROGRAM-BODY-ITER
150   IF N=0 THEN GO TO 260
160   REM*PROCESS-NUMBER-SEL
170   IF N > 0 THEN 210
180   LET C1 = C1 + 1
190   INPUT N
200   GOTO 240
210   REM*PROCESS-NUMBER-OR
220   LET C2 = C2 + 1
230   INPUT N
240   REM*PROCESS-NUMBER-END
250   GOTO 140
260   REM*PROGRAM-BODY-END
270   PRINT "NEGATIVE COUNT ="; C1
280   PRINT "POSITIVE COUNT ="; C2
290   STOP
300   REM*SIGN-COUNT-END
310   END
```

Figure 7.6   *(a) Flat code in COBOL; (b) Flat code in BASIC*

The great disadvantage of flat code is that producing and reading it is not so easy as with hierarchic or nested code. On the other hand it is universally applicable in all programming languages, and the resulting object code tends to run faster and take up less storage space.

JSP preprocessor software packages

The ideal solution to the problem of converting a JSP design into code is to use a software package which converts the program design, formally expressed in some way, into code automatically. There are a number of such packages on the market and they are generally referred to as preprocessors because they convert the design into conventional source code which is then processed by the language compiler like any manually produced source program. This two-stage process is diagrammatically represented in Figure 7.7.

Figure 7.7   *Stages in using JSP preprocessor*

The majority of these packages have been produced for COBOL users, primarily because the majority of JSP users tend to use COBOL as their main programming language. The two most popular of these packages are the JSP-COBOL preprocessor produced by Michael Jackson's own company, Michael Jackson Systems International Limited,[4] and schematic logic preprocessors, of which there are many on the market.

The JSP-COBOL preprocessor accepts a JSP-COBOL program as input. A JSP-COBOL program is divided into four divisions. The first three divisions, the identification, environment and data divisions are coded using the rules of normal COBOL. The procedure division is coded using rules applicable to JSP and is subdivided into two sections, operations and structures. The operations section contains all the executable operations required by the program and is the same as the actions list in JSP except that the actions are written as COBOL statements. The

structures section is a description of the program structure with reference to the operations (i.e. actions) at the places in the structure where they are to be executed. An example of a JSP-COBOL procedure division, for the program design depicted in Figures 7.6 and 7.4, is given in Figure 7.8.

A schematic logic preprocessor is a software package that enables a schematic logic design to be converted into a source program in the target programming language code. One such preprocessor is called SLOGIC, which was developed by the Department of Computation at the University of Manchester Institute of Science and Technology (UMIST).[5] SLOGIC converts a COBOL program whose procedure division has been presented in schematic logic form into conventional COBOL. An example of an SLOGIC procedure division for the schematic logic design presented in Figure 7.4 is given in Figure 7.9.

```
PROCEDURE DIVISION.
OPERATIONS.
1.  STOP RUN.
2.  ACCEPT NUMBER.
3.  MOVE ZERO TO NEGATIVE-COUNT.
4.  MOVE ZERO TO POSITIVE-COUNT.
5.  ADD 1 TO NEGATIVE-COUNT.
6.  ADD 1 TO POSITIVE-COUNT.
7.  DISPLAY "NEGATIVE COUNT =", NEGATIVE-COUNT.
8.  DISPLAY "POSITIVE COUNT =", POSITIVE-COUNT.
STRUCTURES.
SIGN-COUNT SEQ
    DO 3
    DO 4
    DO 2
    PROGRAM-BODY ITR WHILE (NUMBER NOT EQ ZERO)
        PROCESS-NUMBER SEL (NUMBER LESS THAN ZERO)
            DO 5
            DO 2
        PROCESS-NUMBER ALT (ELSE)
            DO 6
            DO 2
        PROCESS-NUMBER END
    PROGRAM-BODY END
    DO 7
    DO 8
    DO 1
SIGN-COUNT END
```

Figure 7.8 *JSP-COBOL procedure division for sign count program*

```
PROCEDURE DIVISION.
SIGN-COUNT SEQ
    MOVE ZERO TO NEGATIVE-COUNT
    MOVE ZERO TO POSITIVE-COUNT
    ACCEPT NUMBER
    PROGRAM-BODY ITER UNTIL NUMBER NOT EQUAL
                                        TO ZERO
        PROCESS-NUMBER SEL NUMBER LESS
                                    THAN ZERO
        ADD 1 TO NEGATIVE-COUNT
        ACCEPT NUMBER
        PROCESS-NUMBER OR NUMBER GREATER
                                    THAN ZERO
        ADD 1 TO POSITIVE-COUNT
        ACCEPT NUMBER
        PROCESS-NUMBER END
    PROGRAM-BODY END
    DISPLAY "NEGATIVE COUNT =", NEGATIVE-COUNT
    DISPLAY "POSITIVE COUNT =", POSITIVE-COUNT
    STOP PROGRAM
SIGN-COUNT END
```

Figure 7.9 *SLOGIC procedure division for sign count program*

Exercises

7.1 The schematic logic in Figure 7.10 represents the design of a program. The actions and conditions in the schematic logic are represented by their numbers from the actions and conditions lists. Draw the skeleton program structure diagram, with allocated actions and conditions, equivalent to this schematic logic.

7.2 Produce the schematic logic equivalent to the detailed program design produced for Exercise 6.1.

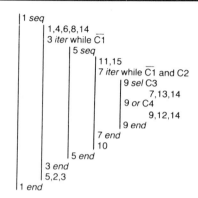

Figure 7.10   *Schematic logic for Exercise 7.1*

8 Structure clashes and program inversion

The programs considered so far have all been 'simple' programs. They have been simple in that a single program structure could be produced by applying the rules of correspondence and matching the data structures relevant to the program. However, in certain situations it is impossible to identify correspondences and hence match the data structures. The situation arising is then referred to as a 'structure clash'. The solution to a structure clash always involves the creation of two or more program routines, each routine being implemented as a subroutine, subprogram or program. There are two common types of structure clash, namely 'sequence clash' and 'boundary clash'.

The first section of this chapter looks briefly at the sequence clash and its resolution. The second section identifies the causes of a boundary clash and how to recognize it. The third and final sections describe two solutions to the boundary clash problem, in the latter section the program inversion technique. In order to understand the implementation of the program inversion technique the reader should have a good understanding of the subroutine concept and the conditional GOTO operation.

Sequence clashes

A sequence clash is present when the lower-level components of one data structure correspond with the lower-level components of another data structure, but are in a difference sequence. This situation usually arises when two or more files are being processed, first serially or sequentially, second simultaneously, and third in different record orders. The problem is best illustrated with the simplest possible example.

Example 8.1 *Sequence clash problem*
An unsequenced version of the job costing file, described in Exercise 4.3, is to be input from punched cards and output in sequence of job code on a printer.

The data structures and apparent correspondences for these two files are given in Figure 8.1. However, although there are the same number of JOB CARDs as JOB CARD IMAGE LINEs, they are not in the same order. A sequence clash has occurred.

The solution to this problem is to split the program into two routines, an input routine and output routine, and:

- either have an intermediate routine which sorts the file into job code sequence;
- or use the input routine to store the file in primary storage, as a table, or in direct-access storage so that the output routine can access the file randomly.

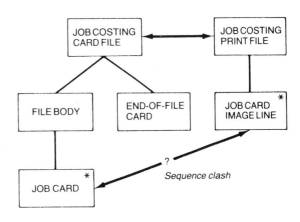

Figure 8.1 *Sequence clash example*

Boundary clashes

Boundary clashes can occur when trying to correspond and match data structures prior to the production of a preliminary program structure. It is best to illustrate the problem through a simple example.

Example 8.2   *Customer sales analysis program*
A program is required which inputs a customer payments file and outputs a customer sales analysis report. The customer payments file contains customer payment records in customer number sequence. Each payment record contains the two data items customer number and payment amount. The paged sales analysis report contains report headings at the top of each page and detail

lines showing each customer payment record and the total of all payments for each customer.

If the sales analysis report were unpaged there would be no difficulty in identifying correspondences and matching the two data structures for this program as can be seen in Figure 8.2.

However, if account is taken of the fact that the sales analysis report is paged, then there is a problem with no correspondences at the middle levels of the data structures, as can be seen in Figure 8.3. It is impossible to match these two data structures and hence form a valid preliminary program structure. The data structures clash with each other and the type of

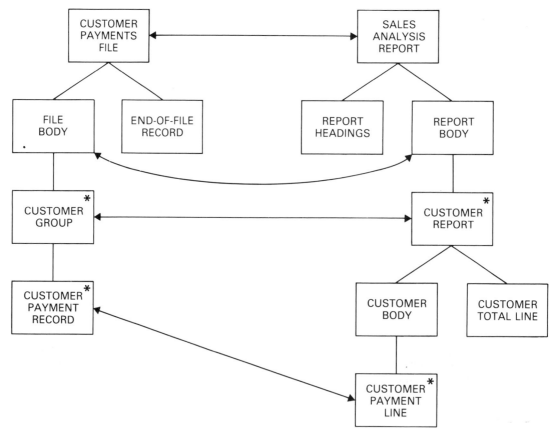

Figure 8.2   *Data structure correspondences for customer sales analysis program when report is unpaged*

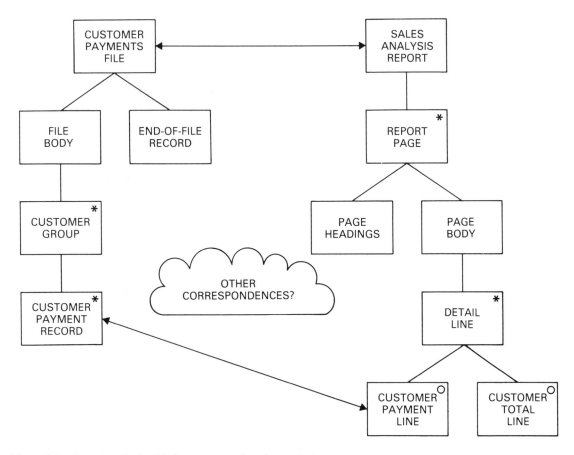

Figure 8.3 *Boundary clash with data structures for sales analysis program*

clash is called a *boundary* clash because, for instance, the boundary of a CUSTOMER GROUP does not coincide with (i.e. clashes with) the boundary of REPORT PAGE or vice versa.

Boundary clashes can occur between the data structures for an input file and an output file, or between two input files or two output files. Two data structures clash if any part of them contains a pair of clashing data components. Usually a boundary clash can be recognized because there is one or more pairs of corresponding components above the clashing components and also one or

more pairs of corresponding components below the clash. The symptom is the existence of two data components which in terms of processing relate together and yet cannot be shown to corrrespond because each is not processed together with a whole number of the other.

For example, a REPORT PAGE is not produced as a result of processing a whole number of CUSTOMER GROUPs.

A case of boundary clash occurs often between an input file and a report file because report pages seldom can be related to the input file.

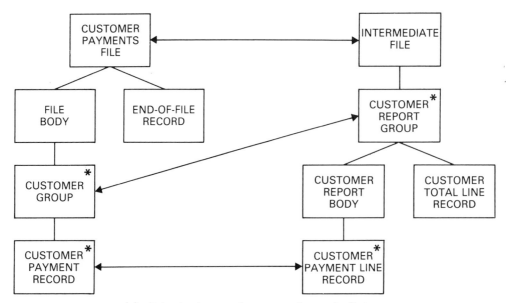

(a)   *Data structures and correspondences for first program*

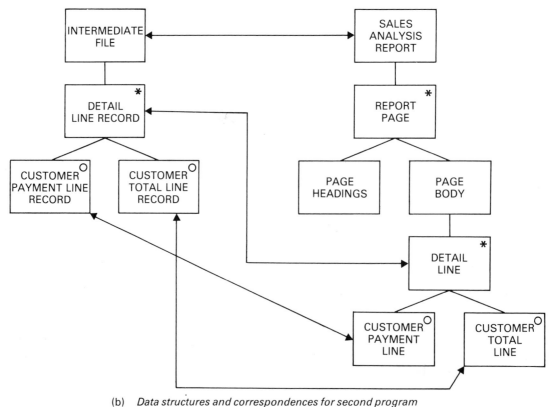

(b)   *Data structures and correspondences for second program*

Figure 8.4   *Resolving boundary clash for sales analysis program using an intermediate file*

Use of an intermediate file to resolve a boundary clash

The boundary clash may be resolved by introducing an intermediate serial file of records each of which is a report detail line. Essentially therefore the problem is being solved by subdividing the program into two. The first program is inputting the customer payments file and creating an intermediate file of report detail line records. The second program is inputting the intermediate file of report detail line records and outputting the paged sales analysis report. The data structures and correspondences for each of these two programs are given in Figure 8.4. (*Note.* The derivation of the intermediate file data structure for the second program assumes a record type code is included in each detail line record to distinguish between customer payment line records and customer total line records.) As can be seen, there is no problem in identifying correspondences for the data structures of these two programs, and hence in forming valid preliminary program structures.

Notice that the logical data structure for the intermediate file will vary, depending on whether it is viewed as the output, for the first program, or the input, for the second program.

A boundary clash, in general, therefore may be resolved by forming two programs linked by an intermediate file. Each record of the intermediate file corresponds to the highest-level data component for which a correspondence exists in both of the clashing structures and which is small enough to be written as a single record.

Use of program inversion to resolve a boundary clash

In the previous section the resolution of the boundary clash was to design two programs with an intermediate file, thus keeping the two clashing data structures separate. However, because the intermediate file has both to be written to and read from perhaps this is not the most efficient solution from a processing point of view. A more efficient solution is to print the report quasi-simultaneously with the processing of the input. To do this we must re-combine the processes of the two programs, using a technique called 'program inversion'.

Program inversion is a technique whereby the intermediate file is discarded, one of the two programs becomes a subroutine of the other, and the 'main' program calls the subroutine every time it would have accessed the intermediate file.

The steps involved in applying the program inversion technique when a boundary clash occurs are as follows:

1   Introduce the intermediate file and design the resulting two programs independently (as described in the previous section) up to and including schematic logic.

2   Decide on the most appropriate inversion, i.e. which of the programs should be the main program and which the subroutine. Usually the output program is chosen as the subroutine.

3   Identify the input/output actions for the intermediate file in the two schematic logic program designs and amend them according to certain rules which are to be described in detail later.

These steps and the rules referred to in step 3 will now be illustrated using Example 8.2.

The data structures for the two programs which use the intermediate file have already been presented in Figure 8.4. The schematic logic which would be derived as a result of applying the complete JSP design method to the two programs is given in Figure 8.5 (overleaf).

The second program will be inverted as a subroutine to the first and hence the first program will become the main program. The input/output actions and conditions for the intermediate file are *indicated in bold fount* in each of the two schematic logics. Amend these I/O operations according to

```
PROGRAM-1 seq
  open customer-payments-file
  open intermediate-file
  read customer-payment-record
  PROGRAM-1-BODY iter while not end-of-customer-payments-file
    set customer-total to zero
    copy customer-number into previous-customer-number
    PROCESS-CUST-BODY iter while
      not end-of-customer-payments-file and customer number
      = previous-customer-number
        set intermediate-record-type to indicate customer-
          payment-line-record
        copy customer-payment-record to customer-payment-
          line-record
        write customer-payment-line-record to intermediate-
          file
        add payment-amount to customer-total
        read customer-payment-record
    PROCESS-CUST-BODY end
    set intermediate-record-type to indicate customer-total-line-
      record
    copy customer-total to customer-total-line-record
    write customer-total-line-record to intermediate-file
  PROGRAM-1-BODY end
  close customer-payments-file
  close intermediate-file
  stop program
PROGRAM-1 end
```

(a)   Schematic logic for first program

```
PROGRAM-2 seq
  open sales-analysis-report
  open intermediate-file
  read intermediate-file-record
  PROCESS-REPORT-PAGE iter while not end-of-intermediate-
  file
    print page-headings
    PROCESS-PAGE-BODY iter while not end-of-intermediate-
    file and not page-full
        PROCESS-DETAIL-LINE sel if customer-payment-line-
          record
            advance 1 line
            write customer-payment-line
            read intermediate-file-record
        PROCESS-DETAIL-LINE or if customer-total-line-record
            advance 4 lines
            write customer-total-line
            read intermediate-file-record
        PROCESS-DETAIL-LINE end
    PROCESS-PAGE-BODY end
  PROCESS-REPORT-PAGE end
  close sales-analysis-report
  close intermediate-file
  stop program
PROGRAM-2 end
```

(b)   Schematic logic for second program

Figure 8.5   *Schematic logic for two programs using intermediate file*

```
INPUT-PROGRAM seq
  open customer-payments-file
  set intermediate-file-switch to zero
  read customer-payment-record
  PROGRAM-BODY iter while not end-of-customer-payments-file
    set customer-total to zero
    copy customer-number into previous-customer-number
    PROCESS-CUST-BODY iter while not end-of-customer-
    payments-file and customer-number = previous-customer-
    number
        set intermediate-record-type to indicate customer-
          payment-line-record
        copy customer-payment-record to customer-payment-
          line-record
        call REPORT-SUBROUTINE using intermediate-
          record-type, customer-payment-line-record,
          intermediate-file-switch
        add payment-amount to customer-total
        read customer-payment-record
    PROCESS-CUST-BODY end
    set intermediate-record-type to indicate customer-total-line-
      record
    copy customer-total to customer-total-line-record
    call REPORT-SUBROUTINE using intermediate-record-
      type, customer-total-line-record, intermediate-file-
      switch
  PROGRAM-BODY end
  close customer-payments-file
  set intermediate-file-switch to 1
  call REPORT-SUBROUTINE using intermediate-record-type,
    null-intermediate-file-record, intermediate-file-switch
  stop program
INPUT-PROGRAM end
```

(a)   Schematic logic for main input program

```
REPORT-SUBROUTINE seq
  go to READ-FIRST-INT-RECORD
    READ-INT-REC-AFTER-PAY
    READ-INT-REC-AFTER-TOT
    depending on entry-status
READ-FIRST-INT-RECORD.
  open sales-analysis-report
  PROCESS-REPORT-PAGE iter while intermediate-file-switch
    = 0
    print page-headings
    PROCESS-PAGE-BODY iter while intermediate-file-
    switch = 0 and not page-full
        PROCESS-DETAIL-LINE sel if customer-payment-line-
          record
            advance 1 line
            write customer-payment-line
            set entry-status to 2
            exit subroutine
READ-INT-REC-AFTER-PAY.
        PROCESS-DETAIL-LINE or if customer-total-line-
          record
            advance 4 lines
            write customer-total-line
            set entry-status to 3
            exit subroutine
READ-INT-REC-AFTER-TOT.
        PROCESS-DETAIL-LINE end
    PROCESS-PAGE-BODY end
  PROCESS-REPORT-PAGE end
  close sales-analysis-report
  exit subroutine
REPORT-SUBROUTINE end
```

(b)   Schematic logic for inverted report subroutine

Figure 8.6   *Implementation of program inversion for sales analysis problem*

the following rules. (The resulting schematic logic for both the main program and inverted subroutine are shown in Figure 8.6.)

(a) To produce the schematic logic for the main program

Instead of writing to the intermediate file a call will be made to the inverted subroutine, passing as parameters an intermediate file record together with an intermediate file switch which will indicate if the intermediate file is open or closed (in order to implement the test of the end-of-file condition of the intermediate file contained in the subroutine).

Hence the detailed changes required to Figure 8.5(a) to produce the schematic logic for the main program are:

1 Replace the action
   open intermediate-file
   by an action to initialize the intermediate file switch
   set intermediate-file-switch to zero
2 Replace all write actions to the intermediate file by a call to the inverted subroutine, passing as parameters the appropriate intermediate file record and the intermediate file switch.
   (a) Replace the action
      write customer-payment-line-record to
         intermediate-file
      by
         call *REPORT-SUBROUTINE*
            using intermediate-record-type,
            customer-payment-line-record and
            intermediate-file-switch
   (b) Replace the action
      write customer-total-line-record to
         intermediate-file
      by
         call *REPORT-SUBROUTINE*
            using intermediate-record-type,
            customer-total-line-record and
            intermediate-file-switch
3   Replace the action
         close intermediate-file
      by the two actions:
         set intermediate-file-switch to 1

call *REPORT-SUBROUTINE*
   using intermediate-record-type, null-
   intermediate-file-record and
   intermediate-file-switch

The first of these actions is setting the intermediate file switch on to indicate that the end of the intermediate file has been reached. The second action is passing this information via the switch parameter to the inverted subroutine, which tests the switch in both of its iterations. Note that the contents of the intermediate file record are irrelevant and hence the use of the word 'null'; the same applies for the intermediate record type.

(b) To produce the schematic logic for the inverted subroutine

Instead of reading from the intermediate file a return is made to the main program to obtain an intermediate file record. On re-entry to the inverted subroutine, after the intermediate file record has been obtained from the main program, it is necessary that the subroutine is executed from the action after the appropriate 'read'. This means inserting a label at each point of exit for a 'read' in the subroutine and including an action at the beginning of the subroutine which will transfer control to the relevant labelled exit in the subroutine. Hence the detailed changes required to Figure 8.5(b) to produce the schematic logic for the inverted subroutine are:

1 Insert the conditional transfer of control action at the beginning of the subroutine. Each of the labels in this action will correspond to each read intermediate file record action.
   go to *READ-FIRST-INT-RECORD*
      READ-INT-REC-AFTER-PAY
      READ-INT-REC-AFTER-TOT
      depending on entry-status
   READ-FIRST-INT-RECORD.
The entry-status indicator is used by the subroutine to remember the last point of exit from the subroutine and to transfer back to that point on re-entry to the subroutine. On first entry to the subroutine (i.e. for the first intermediate file record) the entry-status

indicator will have a preset value of 1 set in the data declarations of the subroutine. Hence on first entry to the subroutine from the main program control will be transferred to the label *READ-FIRST-INT-RECORD.*

2   Remove the action:
>   *open intermediate-file*

and remove the first
>   *read intermediate-file-record*

action because the first call of the subroutine passes the first intermediate file record.

3   Replace each subsequent
>   *read intermediate-file-record*

action by an action which sets the entry-status indicator to a value (2, 3, 4, . . .) which indicates which occurrence of the read it is; plus an exit from subroutine action; plus a label to correspond to the entry point handling code described above.

Hence for the second 'read action' replace by
>   *set entry-status to 2*
>   *exit subroutine*

READ-INT-REC-AFTER-PAY.

and for the third 'read action' replace by
>   *set entry-status to 3*
>   *exit subroutine*

READ-INT-REC-AFTER-TOT.

4   Remove the action
>   *close intermediate-file*

and replace the action
>   *stop program*

by an
>   *exit subroutine*

action.

5   Replace all
>   *not end-of-intermediate-file*

conditions by
>   *intermediate-file-switch = 0*

conditions.

In order to obtain a good understanding of the final detailed design presented in Figure 8.6 the reader is encouraged to 'dry run' the design with some simple test data.

This section has explained the technique of inversion by providing rules that can be applied directly to the schematic logic of the two programs created if an intermediate file is used to solve a boundary clash between two data structures. However, until a good understanding has been obtained of the process of inversion through practice the reader is advised to implement program inversion by firstly coding and testing the two programs separately (i.e. using an intermediate file and not using inversion), and finally, when the two programs are correct, applying the rules to remove the intermediate file by inverting the second program as a subroutine to the first program.

Conversion of JSP design, with inversion, into code

Space does not allow the author to show the programming language code equivalent to the design presented in Figure 8.6 using all of the three languages BASIC, Pascal and COBOL. Hence only the COBOL equivalent, using a subprogram for the inverted subroutine, is shown in Figure 8.7. The complete detailed code is not given in the interests of brevity; however, this should not lead to a loss of understanding for the reader. Note that, because the final design when using program inversion is represented as schematic logic, flat COBOL code is used.

Figure 8.7   *COBOL implementation of program inversion for sales analysis problem (opposite)*

```
IDENTIFICATION DIVISION.
PROGRAM-ID. INPUT-PROGRAM.
        .
        .
        .
ENVIRONMENT DIVISION.
        .
        .
        .
DATA DIVISION.
FILE SECTION.
FD CUSTOMER-PAYMENTS-FILE
        .
        .
        .
WORKING-STORAGE SECTION.
01 INTERMEDIATE-FILE-SWITCH      PIC 9.
01 INTERMEDIATE-RECORD-TYPE      PIC X.
01 CUSTOMER-PAYMENT-LINE-RECORD.
        .
        .
        .
01 CUSTOMER-TOTAL-LINE-RECORD.
        .
        .
        .
01 NULL-INTERMEDIATE-FILE-RECORD.
        .
        .
        .
PROCEDURE DIVISION.
INPUT-PROGRAM-SEQ.
    open customer-payments-file
    MOVE ZERO TO INTERMEDIATE-FILE-SWITCH.
    read customer-payment-record
PROGRAM-BODY-ITER.
    IF end-of-customer-payments-file GO TO PROGRAM-BODY-
        END.
    set customer-total to zero
    copy customer-number into previous-customer-number
PROCESS-CUST-BODY-ITER.
    IF end-of-customer-payments-file OR
        customer-number NOT = previous-customer-number
                        GO TO PROCESS-CUST-BODY-
                        END.
    set intermediate-record-type to indicate customer-payment-line-
        record
    copy customer-payment-record to customer-payment-line-
        record
    CALL REPORT-SUBROUTINE
        USING INTERMEDIATE-RECORD-TYPE, CUSTOMER-
        PAYMENT-LINE-RECORD, INTERMEDIATE-FILE-
        SWITCH.
    add payment-amount to customer-total
    read customer-payment-record
    GO TO PROCESS-CUST-BODY-ITER.
PROCESS-CUST-BODY-END.
    set intermediate-record-type to indicate customer-total-line
    copy customer-total to customer-total-line-record
    CALL REPORT-SUBROUTINE
        USING INTERMEDIATE-RECORD-TYPE, CUSTOMER-
        TOTAL-LINE-RECORD, INTERMEDIATE-FILE-SWITCH.
    GO TO PROGRAM-BODY-ITER.
PROGRAM-BODY-END.
    close customer-payments-file
    MOVE 1 TO INTERMEDIATE-FILE-SWITCH.
    CALL REPORT-SUBROUTINE
        USING INTERMEDIATE-RECORD-TYPE, NULL-
        INTERMEDIATE-FILE-RECORD, INTERMEDIATE-FILE-
        SWITCH.
```

```
    STOP RUN.
INPUT-PROGRAM-END.
```

(a) COBOL main input program (left column)

```
IDENTIFICATION DIVISION.
PROGRAM-ID. REPORT-SUBROUTINE.
        .
        .
ENVIRONMENT DIVISION.
        .
        .
DATA DIVISION.
FILE SECTION.
FD SALES-ANALYSIS-REPORT
        .
        .
WORKING-STORAGE SECTION.
01 ENTRY-STATUS PIC 9 VALUE 1.
LINKAGE SECTION.
01 INTERMEDIATE-FILE-RECORD-TYPE PIC X.
01 INTERMEDIATE-FILE-RECORD      PIC X (120).
01 INTERMEDIATE-FILE-SWITCH      PIC 9.
PROCEDURE DIVISION USING INTERMEDIATE-FILE-RECORD-
                        TYPE, INTERMEDIATE-FILE-
                        RECORD, INTERMEDIATE-FILE-
                        SWITCH.
REPORT-SUBROUTINE-SEQ.
    GO TO READ-FIRST-INT-RECORD,
        READ-INT-REC-AFTER-PAY,
        READ-INT-REC-AFTER-TOT
        DEPENDING ON ENTRY-STATUS.
READ-FIRST-INT-RECORD.
    open sales-analysis-report
PROCESS-REPORT-PAGE-ITER.
    IF INTERMEDIATE-FILE-SWITCH = 1
        GO TO PROCESS-REPORT-PAGE-END.
    print page-headings
PROCESS-PAGE-BODY-ITER.
    IF INTERMEDIATE-FILE-SWITCH = 1
        OR page-full GO TO PROCESS-PAGE-BODY-END.
PROCESS-DETAIL-LINE-SEL.
    IF INTERMEDIATE-FILE-RECORD-TYPE = "T"
        GO TO PROCESS-DETAIL-LINE-OR.
    advance 1 line
    write customer-payment-line
    MOVE 2 TO ENTRY-STATUS.
    EXIT PROGRAM.
READ-INT-REC-AFTER-PAY.
    GO TO PROCESS-DETAIL-LINE-END.
PROCESS-DETAIL-LINE-OR.
    advance 4 lines
    write customer-total-line
    MOVE 3 TO ENTRY-STATUS.
    EXIT PROGRAM.
READ-INT-REC-AFTER-TOT.
PROCESS-DETAIL-LINE-END.
    GO TO PROCESS-PAGE-BODY-ITER.
PROCESS-PAGE-BODY-END.
    GO TO PROCESS-REPORT-PAGE-ITER.
PROCESS-REPORT-PAGE-END.
    close sales-analysis-report
    EXIT PROGRAM.
REPORT-SUBROUTINE-END.
```

(b) COBOL inverted report subroutine

Exercises

8.1   *Batch print program*
An input file consists of batches of records, each batch consisting of a header record followed by one or more detail records (up to approximately 100). Each record in a batch has the same batch number.

The file is terminated by an end-of-file record.

A paged report with report headings at the top of each page is to be produced containing the record images of all the detail records in the file, excluding header records, printed one per line.

You are required to:

(a)   Produce the data structures for the input and report file.

(b)   Identify correspondences between the two data structures, and hence identify the boundary clash.

(c)   Design a solution to the problem which involves an intermediate file and two programs. Express the design of the two programs in schematic logic.

(d)   Implement the solution using program inversion, expressing the designs of the main program and inverted subroutine in schematic logic.

9 Recognition difficulties and backtracking

As described in Chapter 6 it is necessary in many instances when processing an input serial/sequential file to 'read ahead' a record in order to evaluate the condition associated with an iteration or selection. The most common examples of such conditions are 'end of file' and 'change in key'. However, there are instances when reading ahead a single record is not sufficient to evaluate a condition and there is a need to examine many records before a condition may be evaluated. This is an example of a 'recognition difficulty' and it may be resolved as described, by using either the technique of 'multiple read ahead', or the technique of 'backtracking'.

A further type of recognition difficulty occurs when a condition cannot be evaluated because it depends on the results of processing of data which, at the time the condition has to be evaluated, has not yet been done. This type of recognition difficulty can be resolved by also using the backtracking technique. A common problem which leads to this type of recognition difficulty is data validation.

The first section of this chapter describes the multiple read ahead technique which can be used to solve recognition difficulties associated with input data conditions. The second section illustrates the application of the backtracking technique to a simple example. The third section describes the steps of the backtracking technique in detail. The final section concludes the chapter with two examples of the application of the backtracking technique.

Multiple read ahead techniques

As has already been indicated, one type of recognition difficulty can arise when processing one or more input files and the single read ahead technique is not sufficient to allow input conditions associated with iterations and selections to be evaluated. The resolution of this type of recognition difficulty is to read ahead a multiple number of records of an input file, either a fixed number of records or a variable number. These two situations are best illustrated by some simple examples.

Example 9.1 *Program requiring fixed multiple read ahead*
An input file consists of a set of pairs of records, terminated by an end-of-file record. Each pair of records consists of either a type 1 record followed by a type 2 record, or a type 1 record followed by a type 3 record. An output file is to be created from those type 1 records in the input file which are followed by a type 2 record.

There are no difficulties in producing a program structure for this program. The recognition difficulty arises in the resulting detailed design, produced using the procedure defined in Chapter 6, which is depicted in Figure 9.1. The problem arises because of the allocation of the read action. The result of using the single read ahead technique is that on the first execution of the selection component PROCESS PAIR the first type 1 record will just have been read in PROGRAM INITIALIZATION. However, in order to evaluate the conditions associated with the selection component, i.e. whether the second record of the pair is type 2 or 3, the component needs to have available the next record, which it has not. The solution to this problem is quite simple, and it is to use a variation of the read ahead – the multiple read ahead. In the case of Example 9.1 this requires action 6 in Figure 9.1 to be expanded into two actions, 'read first type 1 record' and 'read next record', both actions being allocated to PROGRAM INITIALIZATION.

Similarly action 7 needs to be expanded into two actions, 'read next record' allocated to the two components named PROCESS TYPE 1 RECORD, and 'read next type 1 record'

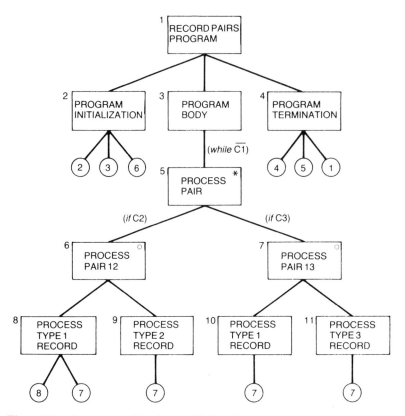

Figure 9.1   *Program requiring fixed multiple read ahead*

allocated to the two components PROCESS TYPE 2 RECORD and PROCESS TYPE 3 RECORD. This application of the multiple read ahead technique of course requires that the type 1 record be safely stored away in primary storage before the second record is read into the input area for the file.

Example 9.1 has illustrated the resolution of a recognition difficulty by the multiple read ahead of a fixed number (i.e. two) of records. The multiple read ahead technique can of course be used to read ahead many records, perhaps using a table or array to store the records, the limitation being the amount of primary storage available.

A situation requiring the multiple read ahead of a variable number of records is illustrated by Example 9.2.

Example 9.2   *Program requiring variable multiple read ahead*

An input file consists of batches of records, each batch consists of one or more detail records terminated by a batch trailer record. The batch trailer record indicates whether the respective batch is of type 1 or type 2. Two output files are to be created, the first to contain all of the type 1 batches from the input file and the second all of the type 2 batches.

Again there are no difficulties in producing a preliminary program structure for this program and allocating conditions as depicted in Figure 9.2. The recognition difficulty arises in the selection component PROCESS BATCH, where the conditions 'Type 1 batch?' and 'Type 2 batch?' cannot be evaluated until the whole batch has been processed and the batch trailer record

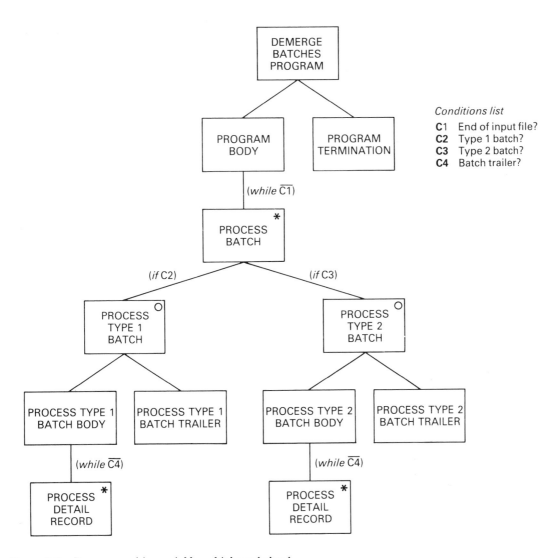

Figure 9.2 *Program requiring variable multiple read ahead*

inspected. There are a number of potential solutions to this problem.

The first potential solution is appropriate if the maximum possible number of detail records in any batch is known, because then a batch may be read ahead into a table. Clearly limitations on the amount of primary storage available for the storage of the maximum possible sized batch may make this solution not feasible.

The second potential solution to this

recognition difficulty is appropriate when the maximum possible number of detail records in any batch either is or is not known. This solution involves reading ahead a batch and storing it temporarily in a work file held on direct access storage.

A third solution to this recognition difficulty which does not involve multiple read ahead is to use a technique called 'backtracking' which is described in the next section.

Backtracking illustrated through a simple example

The backtracking technique is applied to the schematic logic derived from the final program structure with allocated conditions and actions, in particular with read actions implemented using the single read ahead technique. Figure 9.3 depicts the final program structure diagram and resulting schematic logic, using single read ahead for Example 9.2.

The implementation of the backtracking technique as applied to this example will now be explained, the full solution is given in Figure 9.4. Bold font is used to emphasize the changes from Figure 9.3 to Figure 9.4. There are three steps in applying the backtracking technique (see page 118).

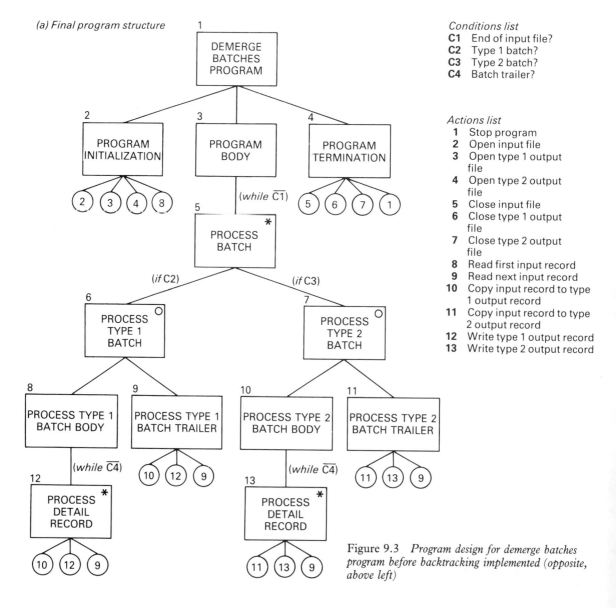

(a) Final program structure

Conditions list
C1 End of input file?
C2 Type 1 batch?
C3 Type 2 batch?
C4 Batch trailer?

Actions list
1 Stop program
2 Open input file
3 Open type 1 output file
4 Open type 2 output file
5 Close input file
6 Close type 1 output file
7 Close type 2 output file
8 Read first input record
9 Read next input record
10 Copy input record to type 1 output record
11 Copy input record to type 2 output record
12 Write type 1 output record
13 Write type 2 output record

Figure 9.3 *Program design for demerge batches program before backtracking implemented (opposite, above left)*

(b) Schematic logic

```
1-PROGRAM seq                                          1-PROGRAM seq
    open input file                                        open input file
    open type 1 output file                                open type 1 output file
    open type 2 output file                                open type 2 output file
    read first input record                                read first input record
    3-PROGRAM-BODY iter while not end of input file        3-PROGRAM-BODY iter while not end of input file
        5-PROCESS-BATCH sel if type 1 batch                    5-PROCESS-BATCH posit type 1 batch
            6-PROC-TYPE-1-BATCH seq                                6-PROC-TYPE-1-BATCH seq
                8-PROC-BODY iter while not batch trailer               open work file
                    copy input record to type 1 output record         8-PROC-BODY iter while not batch trailer
                    write type 1 output record                            copy input record to work record
                    read next input record                                write work record
                8-PROC-BODY end                                           read next input record
                copy input record to type 1 output record             8-PROC-BODY end
                write type 1 output record                            quit 5-PROCESS-BATCH posit if type 2 trailer
                read next input record                                close work file
            6-PROC-TYPE-1-BATCH end                                   open work file
        5-PROCESS-BATCH or if type 2 batch                            read first work record
            7-PROC-TYPE-2-BATCH seq                                   11-PROC-WORK-BODY iter while not end of
                10-PROC-BODY iter while not batch trailer                 work file
                    copy input record to type 2 output record            copy work record to type 1 output record
                    write type 2 output record                           write type 1 output record
                    read next input record                               read next work record
                10-PROC-BODY end                                      11-PROC-WORK-BODY end
                copy input record to type 2 output record            close work file
                write type 2 output record                            copy input record to type 1 output record
                read next input record                                write type 1 output record
            7-PROC-TYPE-2-BATCH end                                   read next input record
        5-PROCESS-BATCH end                                       6-PROC-TYPE-1-BATCH end
    3-PROGRAM-BODY end                                        5-PROCESS-BATCH admit type 2 batch
    close input file                                              7-PROC-TYPE-2-BATCH seq
    close type 1 output file                                          close work file
    close type 2 output file                                          open work file
    stop program                                                      read first work record
1-PROGRAM end                                                         10-PROC-BODY iter while not end of work file
                                                                          copy work record to type 2 output record
                                                                          write type 2 output record
                                                                          read next work record
                                                                      10-PROC-BODY end
                                                                      close work file
                                                                      copy input record to type 2 output record
                                                                      write type 2 output record
                                                                      read next input record
                                                                  7-PROC-TYPE-2-BATCH end
                                                          5-PROCESS-BATCH end
                                                      3-PROGRAM-BODY end
                                                      close input file
                                                      close type 1 output file
                                                      close type 2 output file
                                                      stop program
                                                  1-PROGRAM end
```

Figure 9.4 *Schematic logic for demerge batches program after backtracking implemented*

Step 1   Make an arbitrary choice ('posit')

The recognition difficulty, for the program design in Figure 9.3(b), arises on entry to the selection component 5-PROCESS-BATCH where the conditon 'type 1 batch?' cannot be evaluated because only the first detail record of the batch has been read in, whereas the trailer record is required to evaluate the condition.

The backtracking technique requires that an arbitrary decision be made and an assumption that the condition controlling the selection can be made.

The arbitrary decision made in the solution depicted in Figure 9.4 is to posit (i.e. assume) that the condition 'type 1 batch' is true. This is represented in the schematic logic by changing

> 5-PROCESS-BATCH *sel* if type 1 batch

to

> 5-PROCESS-BATCH *posit* type 1 batch

Step 2   Proceed until choice proved to be right or wrong; if wrong 'quit' and follow alternative choice ('admit')

Having made an arbitrary decision to overcome the recognition difficulty and allowing the program to proceed as if the condition controlling the selection could be made, at some point in the processing it is possible to determine whether the assumption was correct or not. If the assumption was correct then processing may continue as normal. If the assumption was incorrect then the program would want to immediately 'quit' (i.e. leave) the present processing, recover (i.e. 'backtrack') from any incorrect processing done as a result of making the wrong assumption and then 'admit' the assumption was wrong and carry out the correct processing.

The point at which the correctness, or otherwise, of the assumption (i.e. posit) can be evaluated for the solution depicted in Figure 9.4 is on exit from the iteration component 8-PROC-BODY. This requires the insertion of a special 'quit' action immediately following 8-PROC-BODY *end*:

> quit 5-*PROCESS-BATCH posit* if type 2 trailer

The quit action causes an implied transfer of control to the component of the program design which will 'admit' the assumption was wrong and process a type 2 batch. This is represented in the schematic logic by changing

> 5-PROCESS-BATCH *or* if type 2 batch

to

> 5-PROCESS-BATCH *admit* type 2 batch

However, the *admit* component may require actions to recover from incorrect processing (N.B. called 'intolerable side effects'), this is now described in Step 3.

Step 3   Deal with side effects if original choice wrong

Actions arising from intolerable side effects of making the wrong assumption at the *posit* stage have to be identified and dealt with. There are two methods of dealing with side effects:

(a)   *Pretend and really do*

The action giving rise to the side effect is replaced by one which only pretends to do what the action does. The action is then really done at the end of the *posit* component, when the assumption is known to be true. This method is commonly used when the intolerable side effects are concerned with output.

(b)   *Do and undo*

The action giving rise to the side effect is actually done. It is then undone on entry to the *admit* component. This method is commonly used when the intolerable side effects are concerned with input, although it can be used for output side effects. It can be achieved by backspacing files, or the use of temporary work files or the use of tables in primary storage.

The intolerable side effects for Example 9.2 are concerned with both the input and output files, in that a type 2 batch will have been input and processed as a type 1 batch. A backtracking solution to this side effect is to use a temporary work file to hold each output batch until the type of batch can be confirmed.

The changes (shown in bold font) necessary to the schematic logic for this backtracking solution can be seen in Figure 9.4. Figure 9.5 reflects the changes required to the final program structure diagram arising from the changes to the schematic logic required to implement the backtracking

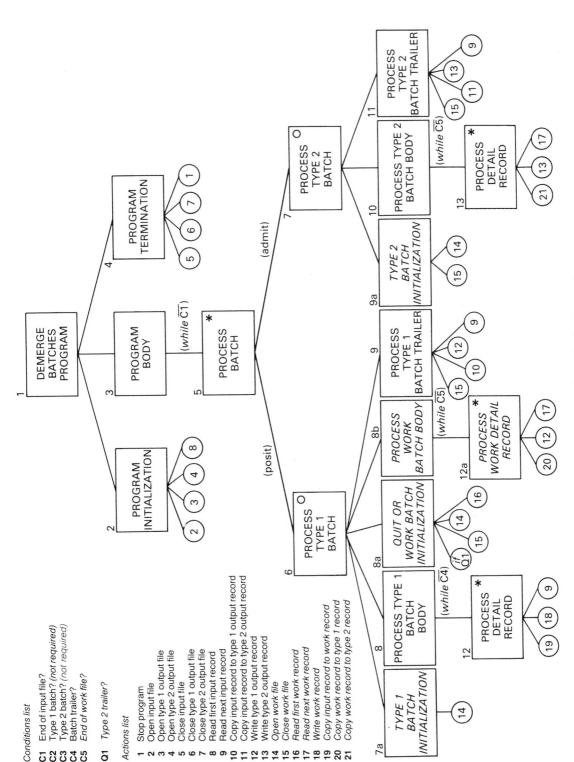

Conditions list

- **C1** End of input file?
- **C2** Type 1 batch? *(not required)*
- **C3** Type 2 batch? *(not required)*
- **C4** Batch trailer?
- **C5** End of work file?

- **Q1** *Type 2 trailer?*

Actions list

1. Stop program
2. Open input file
3. Open type 1 output file
4. Open type 2 output file
5. Close input file
6. Close type 1 output file
7. Close type 2 output file
8. Read first input record
9. Read next input record
10. Copy input record to type 1 output record
11. Copy input record to type 2 output record
12. Write type 1 output record
13. Write type 2 output record
14. Open work file
15. Close work file
16. Read first work record
17. Read next work record
18. Write work record
19. Copy input record to work record
20. Copy work record to type 1 record
21. Copy work record to type 2 record

Figure 9.5 *Program structure diagram for demerge batches program after backtracking implemented*

technique for the solution to Example 9.2. The changes from Figure 9.3(a) to Figure 9.5 are shown in italics. The particular aspects to be noted are (a) the posit–admit component replaces the original selection and is represented in a similar way to a selection except that the words *posit* and *admit* identify the posited and admitted components respectively; (b) the quit condition is identified separately in the conditions list using a Q prefix, and the point at which the condition is tested is indicated on the program structure like an action; and (c) the additional actions required to recover from side effects are added to the actions list. It should be noted that in practice the program components are renumbered rather than using a letter suffix for added components, which is only used in Figure 9.5 to show more clearly the changes from Figure 9.3(a).

A JSP design involving backtracking is converted either into nested code or into flat code and hence the use of the schematic logic representation of the program design is advised. Two of the features arising in a schematic logic design involving backtracking need further explanation as regards conversion to code. First, a posit–admit component is implemented as for a sequence. Second, a conditional quit action is implemented as an IF 'quit condition' THEN GO TO 'admit leg'.

Procedure for backtracking

The previous section has shown the application of the backtracking technique to a specific problem. This section will now describe formally all aspects of the backtracking technique before moving on in the following section to illustrate further the application of the backtracking technique to two other examples.

The backtracking technique is not applied until the final program structure with allocated actions (using single read ahead actions) and conditions has been produced in the normal way. The backtracking technique is applied to the schematic logic equivalent of the final program structure diagram. The potential need for the use of the backtracking technique arises because of identified recognition difficulties, although as described in the first section of this chapter the use of the multiple read ahead technique might lead to an easier solution.

There are three steps in applying the backtracking technique.

Step 1   Make an arbitrary choice ('posit')
At the point at which the recognition difficulty arises make an arbitrary decision and proceed as if the decision controlling the iteration or selection could be made.

Step 2   Proceed until choice proved to be right or wrong; if wrong 'quit' and follow alternative choice ('admit')
Treat the arbitrary decision as an assumption and either assume the condition causing the recognition difficulty is true, for selections and iterations, or assume it false, for selections only. Introduce a quit statement(s) at the point(s) at which the correctness, or otherwise, of the assumption can be evaluated. Hence, if the recognition difficulty is for a selection component the following change occurs in the schematic logic if it is assumed the condition is true:

If necessary a selection of more than two components should be restructured to produce a structure involving only two component selections before carrying out this step. For example:

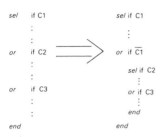

However, if the recognition difficulty is for an iteration component the following change occurs in the schematic logic:

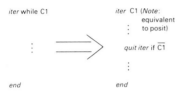

Hence the iteration becomes 'conditionless' and the exit from the iteration is caused by the quit action.

Further examples requiring backtracking

The backtracking technique will now be further illustrated with two examples.

Example 9.3 *Program with recognition difficulty in iteration*

A program is required to input a transaction file and to print the transaction records, one per line, on a paged report. Following the last detail line a summary line is to be printed identifying the number of records in the transaction file.

The schematic logic which would be derived for this program by applying the standard JSP design method is given in Figure 9.6.

The recognition difficulty in this program design arises because the condition 'while not last page' cannot be evaluated on entry to the 3-PROG-BODY iteration. It can only be evaluated when the last detail line has been printed, i.e. when the end of transaction file has been detected.

Figure 9.7 gives the amended schematic logic using backtracking required to overcome the recognition difficulty. Again bold font has been used in both Figures 9.6 and 9.7 to emphasize the

Step 3 Deal with side effects if original choice wrong

Side effects arise out of program actions done after the posit and before the quit when at the quit stage it is realized the wrong assumption has been made. Side effects are classified, according to the treatment they need:

(a) *Intolerable* side effects are those which must be undone because they prevent proper execution of the admit part.

(b) *Beneficial* side effects should be preserved as they would have to be done again in the admit part if they were undone.

(c) *Neutral* side effects are neither intolerable nor beneficial and therefore they may be preserved or undone, whichever is more convenient.

There are two methods of dealing with intolerable side effects and these were described in the previous section of this chapter.

```
1-PROGRAM seq
    open transaction file
    open report
    zeroize transaction count
    read first transaction record
    3-PROG-BODY iter while not last page
        print page headings
        6-PRINT-PAGE iter while same page
            add 1 to transaction count
            copy transaction record to print line
            write print line
        6-PRINT-PAGE end
    3-PROG-BODY end
    4-PRINT-LAST-PAGE-DETAILS iter while not end of transaction file
        add 1 to transaction count
        copy transaction record to print line
        write print line
    4-PRINT-LAST-PAGE-DETAILS end
    write summary line
    close report
    close transaction file
    stop program
1-PROGRAM end
```

Figure 9.6 *Schematic logic BEFORE backtracking applied to iteration*

```
1-PROGRAM seq
    open transaction file
    open report
    zeroize transaction count
    read first transaction record
    3-PROG-BODY iter not last page
        print page headings
        6-PRINT-PAGE iter while same page
            quit iter if end of transaction file
            add 1 to transaction count
            copy transaction record to print line
            write print line
        6-PRINT-PAGE end
    3-PROG-BODY end
    write summary line
    close report
    close transaction file
    stop program
1-PROGRAM end
```

Figure 9.7   *Schematic logic AFTER backtracking applied to iteration*

changes required. The condition 'not last page?' on the 3-PROG-BODY iteration is assumed to be true and a quit action is introduced into the component responsible for processing a transaction record. The effect of this quit is to transfer control to the component following 3-PROG-BODY, i.e. 4-PRINT-LAST-PAGE-DETAILS. However, because this iteration component is controlled by the 'end of transaction file?' condition, which is also the quit condition, effectively the component 4-PRINT-LAST-PAGE-DETAILS is redundant and the transfer of control is to the following component. When backtracking is applied to iterations, side effects are often beneficial or neutral. In this example the side effects, of printing the last page detail lines, are beneficial.

Example 9.4   *On-line stock issues data collection*
An on-line program inputs stock issue transactions from a terminal and stores them in a serial transaction file. Each stock issue transaction consists of a part number followed by a quantity issued. The program validates each data item as it is input and, if the item is found to be invalid, rejects it immediately and requests re-input of the item before requesting the next item to be input. Furthermore, at any stage of the input of a transaction, the terminal operator can cancel the whole of the input associated with the transaction.

It would be helpful to look at the data structure for a stock issue transaction before moving on to the program schematic logic and identifying the recognition difficulty. The data structure is given in Figure 9.8 and it is left to the reader to confirm the correctness of this data structure. It should be obvious that the recognition difficulty is going to result from the topmost selection of this data structure.

The schematic logic which would be derived for the program by applying the standard JSP design method is given in Figure 9.9 (overleaf) and it is again left to the reader to confirm its correctness.

Figure 9.10 (overleaf) gives the amended schematic logic using backtracking required to overcome the recognition difficulty caused by the fact that the condition 'accepted transaction?' associated with the selection 5-PROCESS-TRANS cannot be evaluated at that point. Again bold font has been used in both Figures 9.9 and 9.10 to emphasize the changes required. The condition 'accepted transaction?' is posited to be true and a quit action is introduced at each point in the posited component where it is possible to confirm or deny that the correct assumption has been made, i.e. at each point where the terminal operator may key in input or cancel the transaction. The effect of each quit will be to transfer control to the admitted component if the quit condition is true. As can be seen, much of the original selected component is redundant when converted to its equivalent admitted component.

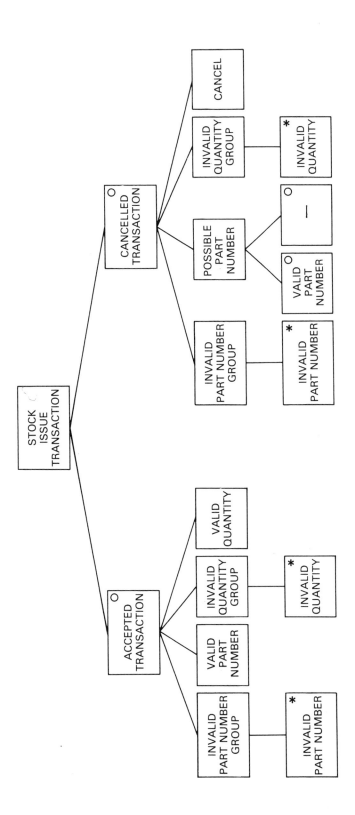

Figure 9.8   *Stock issue transaction data structure*

```
1-PROGRAM seq
    open output transaction file
    input part number
    3-PROG-BODY iter while not end of input transactions
        5-PROCESS-TRANS sel if accepted transaction
            8-PR-INV-PART-GROUP iter while invalid part number
                display error message
                reinput part number
            8-PR-INV-PART-GROUP end
            input quantity
            10-PR-INV-QUANT-GROUP iter while invalid quantity
                display error message
                reinput quantity
            10-PR-INV-QUANT-GROUP end
            write input transaction to output transaction file
            input part number
        5-PROCESS-TRANS or if cancelled transaction
            12-PR-INV-PART-GROUP iter while invalid part
            number or not cancel
                display error message
                reinput part number
            12-PR-INV-PART-GROUP end
            13-PR-POSS-PART-NO sel if not cancel
                input quantity
            13-PR-POSS-PART-NO end
            14-PR-INV-QUANT-GROUP iter while invalid
            quantity or not cancel
                display error message
                reinput quantity
            14-PR-INV-QUANT-GROUP end
            input part number
        5-PROCESS-TRANS end
    3-PROG-BODY end
    close output transaction file
    stop program
1-PROGRAM end
```

Figure 9.9   *Schematic logic for on-line program BEFORE backtracking applied*

```
1-PROGRAM seq
    open output transaction file
    input part number
    3-PROG-BODY iter while not end of input transactions
        5-PROCESS-TRANS posit accepted transaction
            quit posit if cancel
            8-PR-INV-PART-GROUP iter while invalid part number
                display error message
                reinput part number
            quit posit if cancel
            8-PR-INV-PART-GROUP end
            input quantity
            quit posit if cancel
            10-PR-INV-QUANT-GROUP iter while invalid quantity
                display error message
                reinput quantity
            quit posit if cancel
            10-PR-INV-QUANT-GROUP end
            write input transaction to output transaction file
            input part number
        5-PROCESS-TRANS admit cancelled transaction
            input part number
        5-PROCESS-TRANS end
    3-PROG-BODY end
    close output transaction file
    stop program
1-PROGRAM end
```

Figure 9.10   *Schematic logic for on-line program AFTER backtracking applied*

Exercises

9.1   *Name and address program*

A customer name and address (N/A) file contains for each customer four or five records holding the lines of the customer N/A. Each record contains the relevant customer code as well as one of the lines of that customer's N/A. A print program is required to input the customer N/A file and print each customer's N/A as two print lines, with either two N/A lines per print line if it is a four-line N/A or three N/A lines on the first print line and two N/A lines on the second print line if it is a five-line N/A.

You are required to produce the schematic logic for the program:

(a)   as derived after the standard JSP method has been applied;

(b)   after the multiple read ahead technique has been applied:

(c)   after the backtracking technique has been applied.

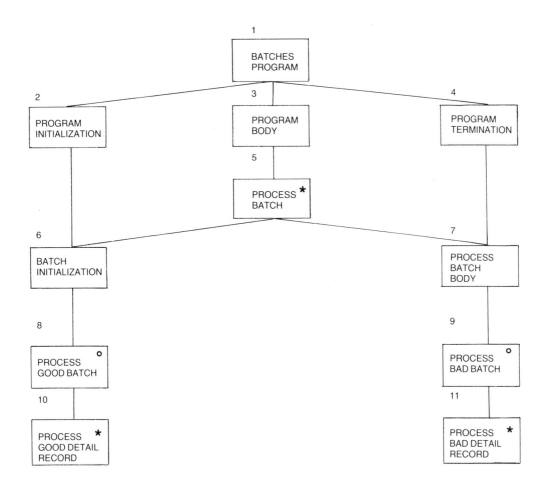

Figure 9.11 *Program structure for batches program before backtracking applied*

9.2 *Batches program*

An input file consists of batches of records. Each batch consists of a header record followed by any number of detail records. The file is terminated by an end-of-file record. An output file is to be created containing all the input detail records from batches whose number of expected detail records, recorded on the batch header record, agrees with the actual number in the batch.

A program structure for this program is given in Figure 9.11. You are required to produce the schematic logic for the program:

(a)   before backtracking is applied;
(b)   after backtracking is applied.

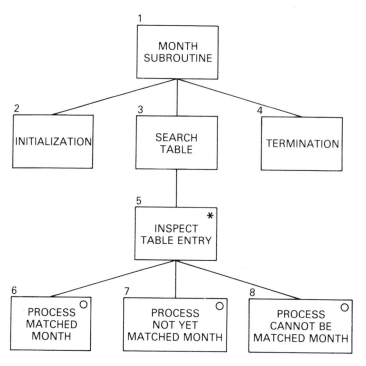

Figure 9.12   *Program structure for month conversion subroutine before backtracking applied*

9.3   *Month conversion subroutine*

A subroutine is required which accepts the name of a month (e.g. MARCH), as an input parameter, and outputs the equivalent month number (e.g. 3), as an output parameter. If the month name is invalid then the month number is set to zero. The subroutine will use a look-up table of month names in month order (i.e. January,

February, March etc.) to translate a month name into a month number.

The JSP program structure for this subroutine is given in Figure 9.12.

You are required to produce the schematic logic for the subroutine:
(a)   before backtracking is applied:
(b)   after backtracking is applied.

10 Beyond design – testing

This chapter examines the impact that JSP can have on program testing and hence its contribution to the correctness of programs. The first section examines the general impact of JSP on the correctness of programs, leading to the particular contribution that JSP can make towards more thorough 'white-box' testing discussed in the remaining sections. The second section describes the derivation of a 'flowschema' from a JSP program structure diagram. The flowschema is a graphical aid which can be used to explicitly identify all the paths through a program. The final section describes the method of identifying test cases from the flowschema.

Achieving correct programs and JSP

For the majority of programmers and programming departments, activity directed at ensuring the correctness of programs takes place late in the program life cycle, usually after the program is designed, coded and compiled free of error. This activity usually consists of running a number of test cases with the program on the computer and is referred to as testing, although perhaps more precisely it should be referred to as machine, or computer, testing.

Machine testing has long been regarded as the 'Cinderella' stage in the program life cycle, being treated as a brief, informal and unimportant exercise to which few resources, both programmer and computer, were allocated. However, in recent years, with the pressures of an ever-increasing maintenance workload (in part due to unreliable programs), and the advent of interactive transaction processing systems (bringing the programs and their errors closer to the user), there has been a greater investment of resources in testing and calls for a more systematic and methodical approach to testing.

Most textbooks define testing along the lines of 'confirmation that a program is correct'. However, this definition suggests that it is possible to prove that any program is correct, i.e. it contains no bugs. There has been a substantial amount of research done on program proving, in which mathematically based techniques have been devised that enable a program to be proved to be correct. However, the techniques are not universally applicable, and also the applicability of the techniques is dependent on the size of the program. An example that is often quoted is that of a Ph.D. student who took eighteen months to prove a 1700-statement program to be correct. With this sort of time and effort it is obvious, at this time in the development of program proving techniques, that other less time consuming, and unfortunately less satisfactory, techniques must be used in trying to achieve correctness.

Testing is therefore not about proving programs to be correct. The only objective that testing can achieve is to demonstrate the presence of bugs, not their absence. Thus the conventional attitude to testing is psychologically wrong. The approach to testing must be to identify the circumstances under which the program does not work, rather than the circumstances under which it does work. The programmer must attempt to maximize the number of times a program goes wrong in order that in the end the correctness of the program is maximized.

So one problem associated with achieving program correctness is the attitude of the programmer in approaching the testing activity. The other problem is the timing; the programmer does not begin to think about bugs and their removal until very late in the program development process. Research that has been undertaken on program bugs has shown that the majority of bugs can be traced back to errors, omissions or ambiguities in the program specification or misinterpretation of the program specification by the programmer. Furthermore this research has shown that the longer a bug remains in a program, the greater the cost for its removal.

Arising out of the discussion so far there are a number of conclusions concerning program bugs; these can be expressed as three simple rules:

Rule 1: avoid them
Rule 2: find them early
Rule 3: find them all.

It is a sobering thought that bugs occur within a program only because the programmer put them there in the first place. What is required, therefore, to avoid the introduction of bugs, is a disciplined, formal and non-intuitive approach to programming. JSP is such an approach; in particular, JSP disciplines the programmer by forcing him to gain a good understanding of the program specification before starting to design the program.

The JSP design method also encourages the early identification of errors, first because it is to a certain extent self-checking, and second because it makes it easier for a third party to check the progress of the program development. It is to a certain extent self- checking because the design method is broken down into a number of well-defined stages where the success of each stage is partly dependent on the previous stage. For instance, difficulty in forming a preliminary program structure may highlight errors in data structures. The control and third-party checking of the programming activity has for a long time been difficult for programming managers to implement. The JSP method makes it more efficient and effective because, first, JSP consists of a number of well-defined stages in which each stage must be carried out with necessary documentation being produced at the end of each stage, and second, given the same problem, a similar solution should be derived by any programmer.

The JSP method also enables a systematic and methodical approach to testing to be applied which leads to more efficient and thorough testing of the program. Furthermore, it enables testing, in particular 'desk checking', to be more easily introduced at an earlier stage in the program development process, from the completion of the program design onwards.

The basic requirement for successful testing is the selection of test data which will maximize the identification of bugs. This will usually require a number of test 'cases' involving different sets of test data.

The first stage in the production of these test cases is the recognition that there are two different views of a program. The first, the 'black box' view is to identify test cases purely from the point of view of the program specification, ignoring the internal workings, i.e. the design of the program. The second, the 'white box' view, is to identify the test cases which exercise every part of the program structure, thus requiring a knowledge of the program's design. It is important that the complete set of test cases should be chosen by taking both the black box and the white box views.

The JSP method cannot directly help the programmer in his black box testing. However, it can indirectly help because the JSP method can lead to a greater understanding of the program specification, and hence to a greater likelihood of the recognition of test cases which will maximize the effectiveness of black box testing. An excellent text on testing, in particular black box, is that entitled *The Art of Software Testing* by G. J. Myers.[6]

White box testing is aimed at ensuring that every combination of actions in the program has been executed at least once, and has the desired effect, and that every condition has been tested with all possible outcomes. This requires that every possible execution path through the program structure has been exercised.

It is in white box testing that the use of JSP can reap the greatest benefits. A JSP program structure diagram, used in conjunction with a graphical aid called a 'flowschema', can be used to explicitly identify all the paths through a program, allowing one test case to be prepared for each.

The flowschema aid described in this book is an adaptation of the flowschema described in the CCA guide no. 9, *Program Validation*.[7]

The steps involved in identifying the white box test cases are as follows:

1 Convert the program structure diagram into a flowschema.
2 Identify each of the unique paths through the flowschema.
3 Derive test data for each of these paths.
4 Derive, from the program specification, expected results for the test data for each of these paths.

Deriving a flowschema

The first step is to convert the program structure diagram into a flowschema using the following rules:

1 *For a sequence.* A sequence in the program structure diagram is converted, in the flowschema, into a single execution path annotated by the component numbers, as illustrated by the example in Figure 10.1.
2 *For a selection* (involving simple conditions or compound conditions with only ANDs). A selection is converted into an execution path which subdivides into an appropriate number of subpaths equal to the number of selected child components as illustrated by the example in Figure 10.2.

Note that the head of each subpath is annotated with the condition which dictates whether that path is selected, and that the flowschema construct is explicitly shown to arise from a selection by the use of the selection symbol (○) at the point of subdivision of the path.
3 *For an iteration* (involving a simple condition only) there are two types of iteration, 'zero based' and 'non-zero based' each of which is represented slightly differently in the flowschema. The representation of each will be illustrated with the example of an iteration given in Figure 10.3.

The representation of a zero based version of this iteration, i.e. one where the iterated child component may not be executed at all, is as depicted in Figure 10.4 (overleaf).

This example illustrates that there are two paths through the iteration. The first is when the iterated child component 2 is executed at least once, and the second is when component 2 is not executed at all. Note that again, as

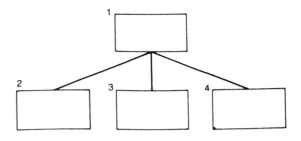

Program structure diagram

Flow schema

Figure 10.1   *Flowschema for sequence*

with the selection, the condition that dictates if a path is executed is annotated at the head of the respective subpath.

In the case of the path in which the iterated component is executed at least once, the condition for exit from the iteration is annotated at the end of the respective subpath. Note also that the flowschema construct is explicitly shown to arise from an iteration by the use of the iteration symbol (★) at the point of the subdivision of the path.

The representation of a non-zero based iteration, i.e. one where the iterated child

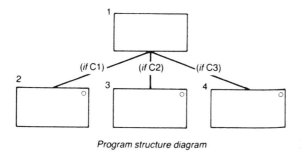

Program structure diagram

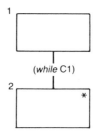

Figure 10.3   *Iteration component*

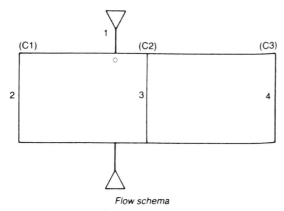

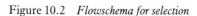

Flow schema

Figure 10.2   *Flowschema for selection*

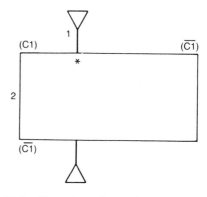

Figure 10.4   *Flowschema for zero based iteration*

component must be executed at least once, is illustrated in Figure 10.5.

This example illustrates that there is only one path through the iteration which involves the execution of the iterated component numbered 2 at least once.

4   *Produce flowschema 'in–outwards'.* In deriving the flowschema the best approach is to convert the program structure 'bottom up' and hence produce the flowschema 'in–outwards'. This means that for the sign-count program, whose program structure diagram is given in Figure 10.6, the part of the flowschema for the selection is drawn first. This is then enhanced by adding that part representing the iteration, and finally the flowschema is completed by adding that part representing the sequence.

If these rules are applied to the sign-count program structure diagram of Figure 10.6, then the equivalent flowschema are derived in stages as depicted in Figure 10.7. It should be noted that

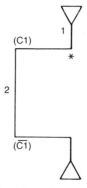

Figure 10.5   *Flowschema for non-zero based iteration*

the use of squared paper can ease the task of drawing a flowschema.

The rules described so far for deriving a flowschema are applicable only for a program structure involving simple conditions and selections involving compound conditions with ANDs. The procedure is more complicated if the program structure involves compound conditions with ORs.

In producing the flowschema for a program

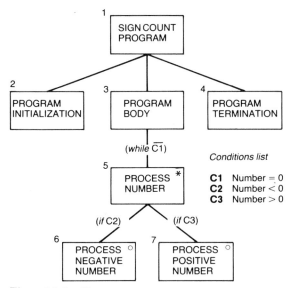

Figure 10.6 *Sign count program structure*

Conditions list

C1 Number = 0
C2 Number < 0
C3 Number > 0

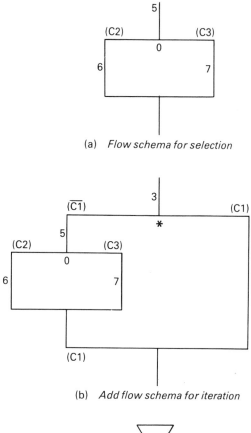

(a) *Flow schema for selection*

(b) *Add flow schema for iteration*

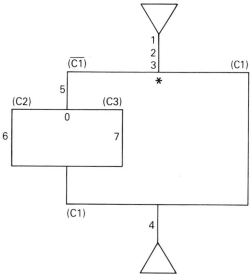

(C) *Add flow schema for sequence to complete flow schema*

structure involving ORed compound conditions the parts of a compound condition which are ORed together must be treated as separate conditions leading to separate paths in the flowschema. In looking at compound conditions you should remember that, if necessary, De Morgan's law should be applied to simplify the compound condition.

The procedure for dealing with selections and iterations involving ORed compound conditions is as follows:

1 *Selections (with ORed compound conditions).*
Consider the selection component in Figure 10.8 (overleaf). The left leg of the selection is dependent on a condition which consists of three ORed parts, i.e. C1, C2 and (C3 AND C4), and hence this results in three paths associated with that leg. Using De Morgan's theorem the right leg condition simplifies to $\overline{C1}$ AND $\overline{C2}$ AND ($\overline{C3}$ OR $\overline{C4}$) and hence consists of two ORed parts, i.e. ($\overline{C1}$ AND $\overline{C2}$ AND $\overline{C3}$) and ($\overline{C1}$ AND $\overline{C2}$ AND $\overline{C4}$). This leads to two paths associated with the right leg of the selection. Hence the number of paths

Figure 10.7 *Derivation of flowschema for sign count program (right)*

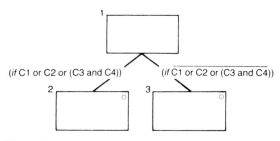

Figure 10.8   *Selection component with ORed compound conditions*

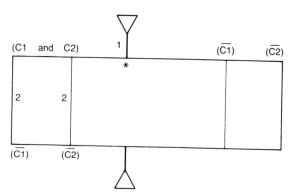

Figure 10.11   *Flowschema for zero based iteration involving ORed condition*

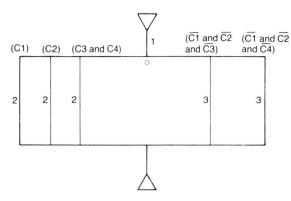

Figure 10.9   *Flowschema for selection component with ORed conditions*

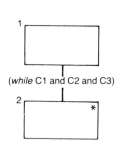

Figure 10.12   *Non-zero based iteration*

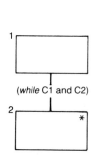

Figure 10.10   *Zero based iteration*

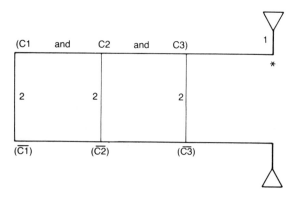

Figure 10.13   *Flowschema for non-zero based iteration involving ORed condition*

through the selection is five and the flowschema for this selection is as in Figure 10.9 (overeleaf).

2   *Zero based iterations (with compound conditions).* Consider the zero based iteration of Figure 10.10 (overleaf). The negative of the condition associated with the iteration, required for exit from the iteration is $\overline{C1 \text{ AND } C2}$. Using De Morgan's theorem this simplifies to $\overline{C1} \text{ OR } \overline{C2}$ and hence consists of two ORed parts, i.e. $\overline{C1}$ and $\overline{C2}$. In the flowschema representation of the iteration, therefore, this leads to four possible paths through the iteration component, as depicted in Figure 10.11 (overleaf).

3   *Non-zero based iterations (with compound conditions).* Consider the non-zero based iteration of Figure 10.12 (overleaf). The negative of the condition associated with the iteration is $\overline{C1 \text{ AND } C2 \text{ AND } C3}$, which simplifies to $\overline{C1} \text{ OR } \overline{C2} \text{ OR } \overline{C3}$ and hence consists of three ORed parts, i.e. $\overline{C1}, \overline{C2}, \overline{C3}$. In the flowschema representation of the non-zero based iteration this leads to three possible paths through the iteration component, as in Figure 10.13.

4   *Mixed mode iterations.* If the condition associated with the exit from an iteration is an ORed compound condition, it is possible that one or more parts of the condition can lead to a zero occurrence of the child component and

one or more parts can lead to a non-zero occurrence.

Consider the iteration of Figure 10.12. The exit condition for this iteration is $\overline{C1} \text{ OR } \overline{C2} \text{ OR } \overline{C3}$. If a zero occurrence can arise only with condition $\overline{C1}$, then the flowschema representation of this iteration is as depicted in Figure 10.14.

Hence the number of paths through this iteration component is four.

The above rules can be illustrated with the following example.

Example 8.1   *Stores movements program*
An analysis of a stores movements file is required. The stores movements file contains records, each of which includes the following data items: part number, movement type (issue or receipt), quantity issued or received (positive number). The stores movements records have been validated and sorted into part number sequence and are terminated by an end-of-file record. The analysis report is to be produced on a printer with the following specification: heading line (top of first page) followed by part number reports (one for each part number, containing the part number and the total net movement for the part) followed by a summary line (at the end of the report, and containing the total number of issue records and the total number of receipt records). The report flows heedlessly over any perforations in the printer paper.

The program structure, with allocated conditions, for this example is given in Figure 10.15 (overleaf). You should note in particular that component 7 is a completely non-zero based iteration in that, on first entry to this iteration, condition C1 cannot be true and condition C2 must be true. Hence the flowschema for this program is as depicted in Figure 10.16 (overleaf).

The only remaining type of program component for which the derivation of its flowschema equivalent has not been described is the posit–admit construct for backtracking.

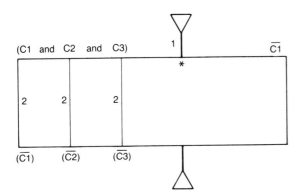

Figure 10.14   *Flowschema for mixed mode iteration involving ORed condition*

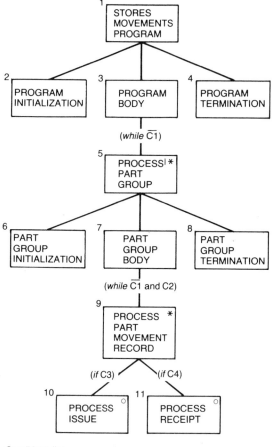

Conditions list

C1 End of stores movement file?

C2 Previous part number = present part number?

C3 Movement type = issue?

C4 Movement type = receipt?

Figure 10.15　*Program structure for stores movements program*

A posit–admit construct arising from a selection should be drawn in a flowschema as if it were a normal selection. Each QUIT is then inserted in the flowschema as a selection at the point at which it occurs in the structure. However, since satisfaction of the QUIT condition causes a jump, one side of the QUIT selection should be closed off with the reference of the ADMIT leg enclosed in a triangle, as shown in Figure 10.17 (overleaf).

A posit–admit construct arising from an iteration should be drawn in a flowschema as if it were a normal iteration. Figure 10.18 (p. 136) gives the program structure equivalent to the schematic logic given in the solution to Example 9.3 in Figure 9.7 and the equivalent flowschema. The conditional QUIT is again inserted in the flowschema as a selection at the point at which it occurs in the structure. Figure 10.19 (p. 137) gives the program structure equivalent to the schematic logic given in the solution to Exercise 9.3(b) and the equivalent flowschema. It should be noted that in this example there are two unconditional QUITs to the end of the iteration.

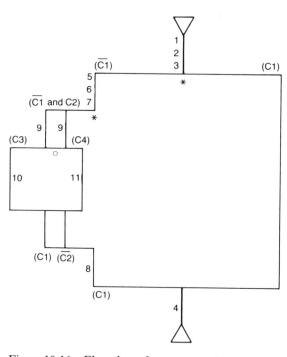

Figure 10.16　*Flowschema for stores movements program*

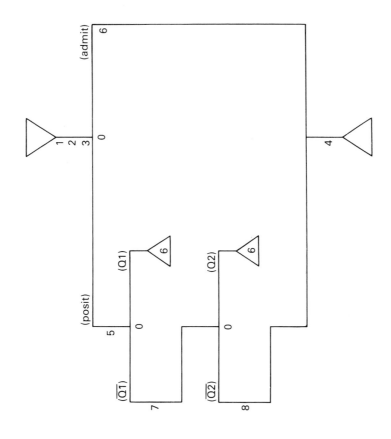

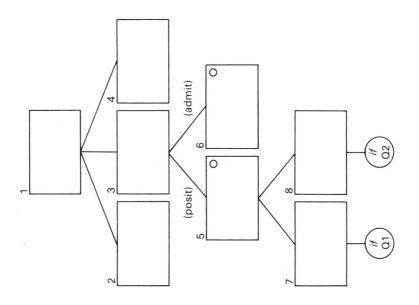

Figure 10.17   *Flowschema for backtracking*

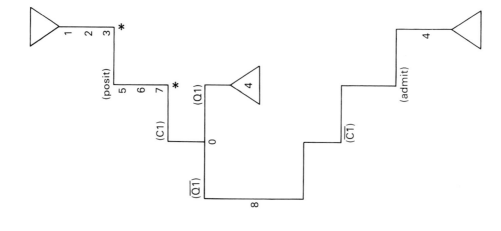

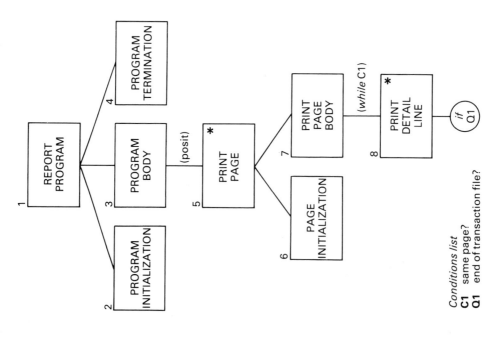

Conditions list
C1 same page?
Q1 end of transaction file?

Figure 10.18   *Program structure and equivalent flowschema for report program with backtracking applied to iteration*

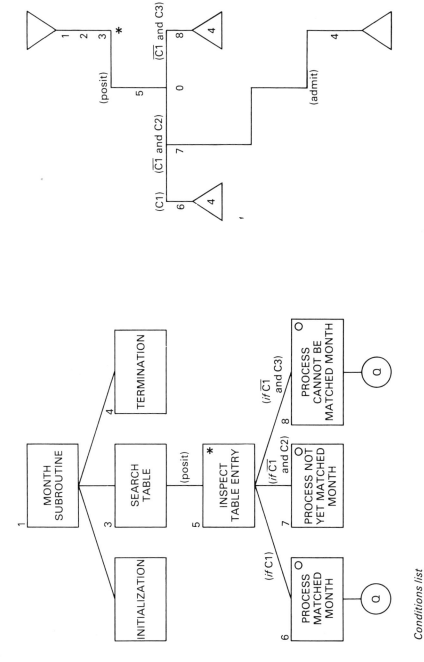

Figure 10.19 *Program structure and equivalent flowschema for month conversion subroutine*

Conditions list
C1 month–name = month-table (subscript)?
C2 subscript < 12
C3 subscript = 12
(Q is an unconditional quit)

Deriving test paths and cases

Having produced a flowschema, we next identify each of the unique paths through it. Each path is best represented by listing the conditions that determine the execution of that path. It should be remembered that, for paths involving the execution of an iterated component at least once, the negative of the condition must eventually exist to leave the iteration component. This is denoted in the list of conditions representing that path by enclosing the condition for leaving the iteration in brackets. Hence for the flowschema for the sign-count program given in Figure 10.7 the paths are identified as illustrated in Figure 10.20 and for the flowschema for the stores movements program given in Figure 10.16 the paths are identified as illustrated in Figure 10.21.

Test path no.	Path conditions
1	$\overline{C1}$, C2, (C1)
2	$\overline{C1}$, C3, (C1)
3	C1

Figure 10.20   *Test paths for sign count program*

Test path no.	Test path conditions
1	$\overline{C1}$, $\overline{C1}$ and C2, C3, (C1), (C1)
2	$\overline{C1}$, $\overline{C1}$ and C2, C4, (C1), (C1)
3	$\overline{C1}$, $\overline{C1}$ and C2, C3, ($\overline{C2}$), (C1)
4	$\overline{C1}$, $\overline{C1}$ and C2, C4, ($\overline{C2}$), (C1)
5	C1

Figure 10.21   *Test paths for stores movements program*

Having identified the test paths the final step is to identify the characteristics of the test data which will ensure that each test path is exercised. This requires for each test path an identification of the minimum test data which will cause the conditions of the test path conditions list to become true in the order specified by the list.

It should be noted that for test paths involving iterations the minimum test data may need to exercise the iterated component more than once. This applies, for instance, in the case of test paths 3 and 4 in Figure 10.21 where the inner iteration controlled by the exit condition (C2) needs to be exercised more than once in order to exit from the outer iteration controlled by the exit condition (C1). It also applies to iterations where the iterated component has to be executed a fixed number of times.

Also it should be noted that some test paths identified may be impossible because a particular sequence of conditions is impossible. For instance the following test path:

$\overline{C1}$, $\overline{C1}$ and C2, $\overline{C1}$ and C2 and C3, (C1), ($\overline{C2}$), (C1)

where C1 end of file?
        C2 same department?
        C3 same employee?

is impossible because once C1 is true in the innermost iteration it is impossible for $\overline{C2}$ to be true for the next iteration.

A test case consists of a description of the minimum test data required to exercise a test path together with a prediction of the expected results. For each test path therefore the expected results for the test data should be identified using the program specification.

The test cases for the sign-count program and stores movements program are depicted in Figures 10.22 and 10.23 respectively.

Test path	Minimum test data	Expected results
1	Negative number followed by zero number	Positive count=0, negative count=1
2	Positive number followed by zero number	Positive count=1, negative count=0
3	Zero number	Positive count=0, negative count=0

Figure 10.22   Test cases for sign count program

Test path	Test data	Expected results
1	Issue record, followed by end-of-file record	One part number report, net movement = quantity issued from issue record; one summary line, number of issue records = 1 number of receipt records = 0 etc.
2	Receipt record, followed by end-of-file record	
3	Two issue records with different part numbers, followed by end-of-file record	
4	Two receipt records with different part numbers, followed by end-of-file record	
5	End-of-file record	

Figure 10.23   *Test cases for stores movements program*

Exercises

10.1   *Job costing program (second version)*
For the detailed design produced for Exercise 6.2:
  (a)   produce the test flowschema;
  (b)   identify the unique test paths through the flowschema;
  (c)   identify test data.

10.2   *Batches program*
This exercise relates to Exercise 9.2 from the previous chapter. Figure 10.24 (overleaf) depicts the program structure equivalent to the schematic logic given in the solution to Exercise 9.2(b). You are required to:
  (a)   produce the test flowschema;
  (b)   identify the unique test paths through the flowschema.

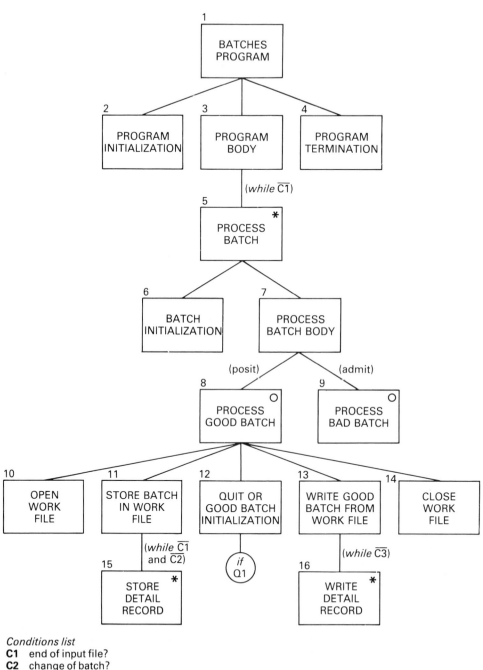

Figure 10.24   *Program structure for batches program after backtracking applied*

11 Network database programs and JSP

The JSP design method is based upon a hierarchical view of the data processed by a program. This is an acceptable view for programs that process conventional files. However, what happens if the data being processed by a program is stored non-hierarchically, which is true for instance in many databases, e.g. a Codasyl network database supported by IDMS? The first section of this chapter explains, using an example, the differences between holding data in hierarchical conventional files and a network database. The second section explains that a program's logical view of a network database can be described in terms of a database navigation structure diagram. The final section describes the impact of database conditions on the JSP data base navigation structure and hence the resulting final program design. It should be noted that the reader should have a good understanding of Codasyl network databases before attempting to read this chapter.

Hierarchical vs. non-hierarchical structures

The JSP data structures that have been used so far have all been strictly hierarchical – they are tree structures, in which there is only one path from the root component to a given node. This is to be expected as conventional files are hierarchical organizations of data. Figure 11.1 (overleaf) shows the JSP hierarchical data structure from Figure 3.22 and its corresponding tree structure representation.

Consider an example of the data involved in a college timetabling system. A number of entities need to be represented in this data together with various relationships between the entities. Examples of these entities and their relationships are:

Entities
1 class
2 lecturer
3 student
4 course
5 room

Relationships
1 a CLASS is taught by a LECTURER to a COURSE in a ROOM.
2 a LECTURER teaches many CLASSes.
3 a COURSE consists of many STUDENTs.
4 a ROOM is used by many CLASSes.
5 a COURSE is taught by many LECTURERs.

If the college timetabling system uses conventional hierarchical data files, then its data is likely to be held in a number of different master files. Each of these files would have a hierarchical physical structure as illustrated in Figure 11.2 (p. 143) which gives the JSP representation of some of the possible files.

If, however, the college timetabling system uses a non-hierarchical database such as IDMS, which is a 'network' database, then the use of JSP data structure diagrams to represent the physical structure of the database is inappropriate. Luckily database experts have an appropriate diagrammatic method for representing the physical structure of a network database called a Bachman diagram. Figure 11.3 (p. 144) illustrates the Bachman diagram for the college timetabling system's data and relationships.

Each box in the Bachman diagram symbolizes a type of record (which holds data). The lines show relationships between the records. A line always has an arrow pointing to the more frequent records. Thus for each COURSE there are many CLASSes and for each CLASS a single COURSE. All relations are one-to-many and are called *sets*.

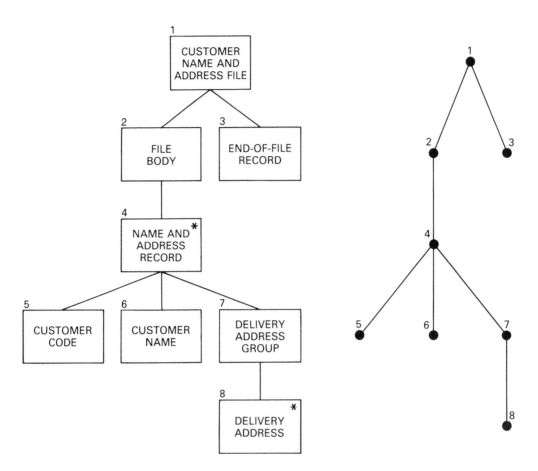

Figure 11.1   *JSP data structure and its equivalent tree structure*

Note: This is not the same as a JSP data structure diagram because:

1   it is a network rather than a tree;
2   every box must represent a record – boxes do not show sets;
3   the lines and arrows show sets of data records.

If JSP hierarchical data structure diagrams cannot be used to represent the physical structure of a network database, does this mean therefore that JSP is inappropriate in designing programs which process such databases?

The answer to this question is no, the use of JSP *is* appropriate in designing programs which process network databases. Whereas JSP data structures are inappropriate in representing the *physical* structure of a network database, they are appropriate in representing the *logical* view that a program has when processing a network database, i.e. in representing the 'database navigation structure' (or 'database access path') for a particular program.

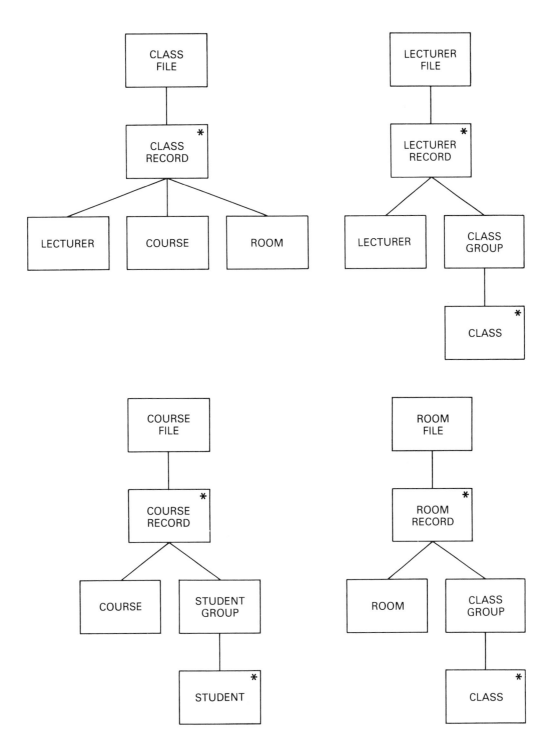

Figure 11.2   *JSP physical data structures for college timetabling system master files*

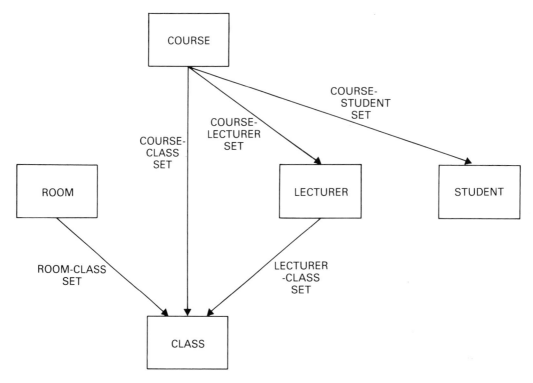

Figure 11.3   *Bachman diagram for college timetabling system*

Database navigation structures and JSP

The actual data records in the Codasyl network database can be organized into chains, each occurrence of a set comprising one chain. For example an occurrence of the COURSE-LECTURER set might be as depicted in Figure 11.4. The diagram could then be expanded to show an occurrence of the LECTURER-CLASS set as shown in Figure 11.5 (p. 146).

From an owner it is always possible to find the first member of a set. How efficient this is depends on the physical storage of the data. It is also possible to find the next member in a set after the current one. Sometimes a database allows the prior (previous) member to be found and for a short cut to be taken to the owner. Another option is a pointer to the last member of a set. In addition some record types may be accessible directly if the

key is known (i.e. via CALC), and not via a set. There will be many access paths through a database, but only a few are an efficient way of solving a problem.

Database programmers are provided with a description of the physical characteristics of the data base by means of a database subschema and its associated Bachman diagram. One of the basic principles of JSP is that the starting point for any program is a logical view of the data for that particular application. It is this logical view which leads to the production of a JSP data structure. Therefore, when accessing a database, the Bachman diagram is used to deduce the most suitable access path through the database to meet the processing requirements of the program. This access path can be expressed using JSP data

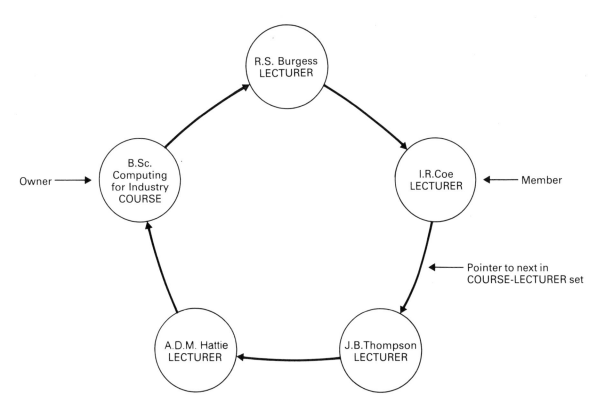

Figure 11.4 *An occurrence of COURSE-LECTURER set*

structure notation and is normally referred to as the 'database navigation structure'.

Let us take a simple example from the college timetabling system. A program is required to produce the names of all lecturers teaching on a specified course. Assuming each COURSE record is a CALC record and each LECTURER record can be accessed VIA the COURSE-LECTURER set, the JSP data base navigation structure is as depicted in Figure 11.6 (p. 147).

Once the database navigation structure for a program has been determined together with any other data structures associated with the program, the usual sequence of events for JSP can be followed and correspondence, preliminary program structure, actions and conditons, and final program structure can be produced.

For the example just discussed there are three data structures: the database navigation structure just defined, the data structure for the input of the course and that for the output of the names of the lecturers. The final program structure is as depicted in Figure 11.7 (p. 147). Notice that the read ahead principle is still appropriate.

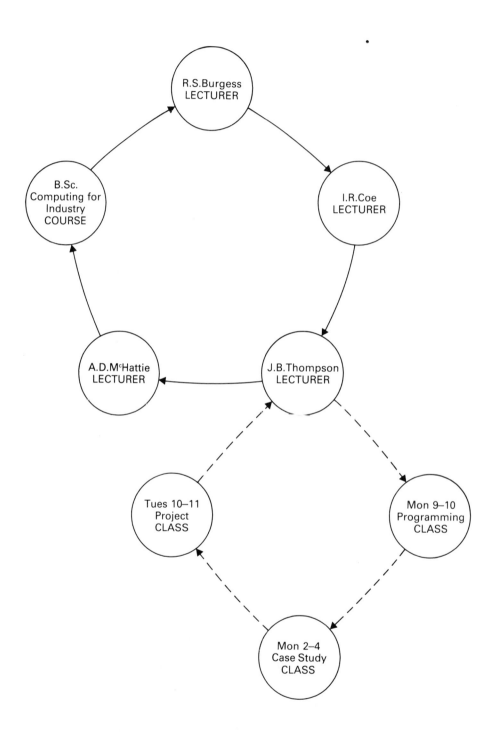

Figure 11.5   *An occurrence of COURSE-LECTURER set with an occurrence of LECTURER-CLASS set*

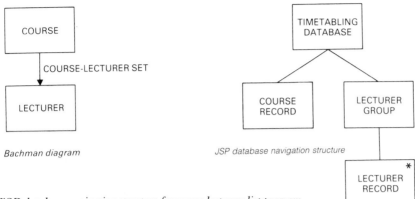

Figure 11.6   *JSP database navigation structure for course lecturers list program*

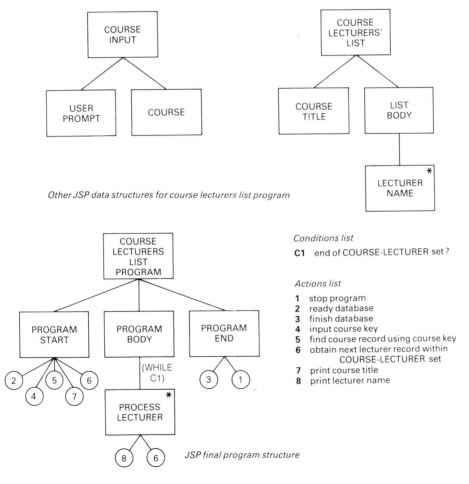

Figure 11.7   *JSP design for course lecturers list program*

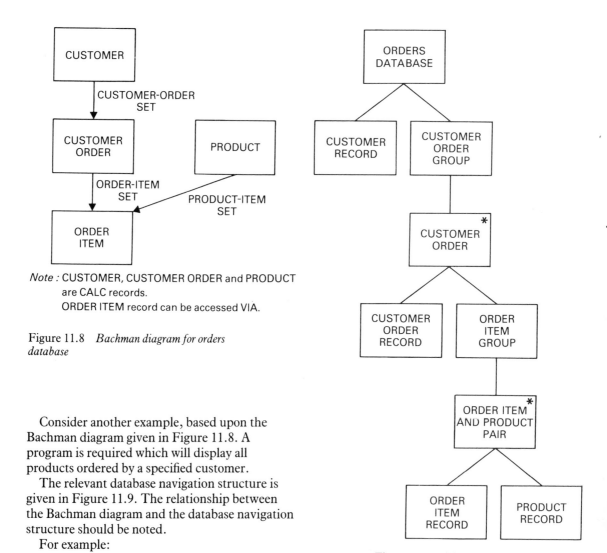

Note : CUSTOMER, CUSTOMER ORDER and PRODUCT are CALC records.
ORDER ITEM record can be accessed VIA.

Figure 11.8   *Bachman diagram for orders database*

Consider another example, based upon the Bachman diagram given in Figure 11.8. A program is required which will display all products ordered by a specified customer.

The relevant database navigation structure is given in Figure 11.9. The relationship between the Bachman diagram and the database navigation structure should be noted.

For example:

Figure 11.9   *JSP database navigation structure for products ordered by customer program*

Navigation structure data component	Bachman diagram records and sets
CUSTOMER ORDER GROUP	All occurrences of ORDER-ITEM set for specified CUSTOMER record *plus* for each ORDER ITEM record, its corresponding PRODUCT record.
ORDER ITEM GROUP	All occurrences of ORDER ITEM record for a specific CUSTOMER ORDER record *plus* for each ORDER ITEM record, its corresponding PRODUCT record.

Database conditions and JSP

A Codasyl database system such as IDMS sets a register known as DB-STATUS whenever a database command has been executed. This register can be tested by the program for such exception conditions as:

> end of realm?
> end of set?
> set not found?
> record not found?
> command unsuccessful?

The second of these conditions has already been used in the example given in Figure 11.7.

Furthermore, IDMS provides a number of explicit conditions which may be used in conjunction with the IF statement, e.g. for COBOL

> *IF* set-name *IS [NOT] EMPTY*

The database navigation structure for the example in Figure 11.7 may be further enhanced by taking into account some of these conditions, which may arise as depicted in Figure 11.10.

Many of the values which can arise in the DB-STATUS register frequently result from hardware or software errors.

It is not normally possible to cater for these errors in the program. Therefore it is important to test the register after each database command has been executed, because if an unexpected error condition is met the program may abandon. However, usually the programmer wishes the program to branch to a particular error routine. By testing the register after each command, database navigation and error routine branching can be successfully achieved.

'Abnormal' values of the register can be catered for in a navigation structure by introducing a selection at the highest level in the structure, as illustrated in Figure 11.11 (overleaf) for the JSP database navigation structure for the course lecturers list program. However this will introduce a recognition problem into the resulting program structure, and hence the selection will require a POSIT and ADMIT, and after every

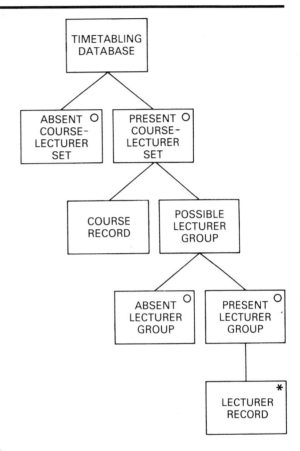

Figure 11.10   *Enhanced JSP database navigation structure for course lecturers list program*

database command action a QUIT relating to the register will be needed.

This is quite straightforward, but care must be taken in positioning the QUIT when a 'normal' condition is to be tested. It has been found to be best to test the normal condition first and then place the QUIT at the next logical point in the structure. This is illustrated in Figure 11.12 (overleaf) by the schematic logic equivalent of the database navigation structure given in Figure 11.11 and further illustrated in Figure 11.13 (overleaf) by the schematic logic equivalent of the lower-level iteration.

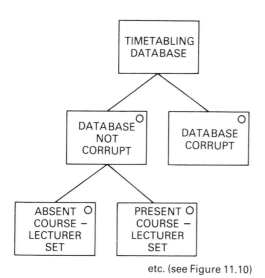

Figure 11.11   *Further enhanced JSP database navigation with abnormal error conditions for course lecturers list program*

etc. (see Figure 11.10)

```
PROGRAM posit  data base not corrupt
                   ready data base
                   input course-key
                   find course-record using course-key
                   POSS-LECT-GR sel if course-record-not-found
                              ⋮
                   POSS-LECT-GR or  if course-record-found
                                  quit PROGRAM posit if command-unsuccessful
                              ⋮
                   POSS-LECT-GR end
                   finish data base
                   stop program
PROGRAM admit data base corrupt
                   (error routine)
PROGRAM end
```

Figure 11.12   *Schematic logic arising from Figure 11.11*

```
   ⋮
obtain next lecturer-record within COURSE-LECTURER set
PRES-LECT-GR iter while not end of COURSE-LECTURER set
                       quit PROGRAM posit if command-unsuccessful
                       print lecturer -name
                       obtain next lecturer-record
PRES-LECT-GR end
   ⋮
```

Figure 11.13   *Schematic logic for iteration*

Exercises

The exercises for this session are based upon the Bachman diagram given in Figure 11.14, which gives full details of the records and sets of a personnel database.

11.1 *Project team members with job title module*
Produce the JSP database navigation structure for a program module which, given a specified job title and project

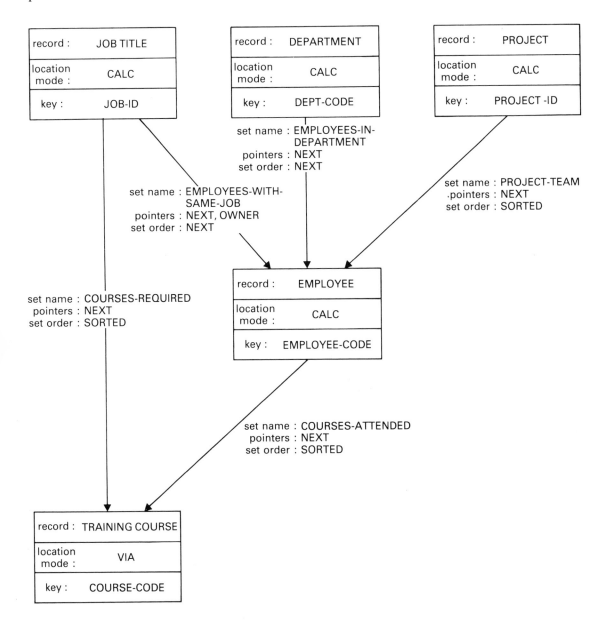

Figure 11.14 *Bachman diagram for personnel database*

identification, calculates the number of employees in the project team who have that job title. Ignore database corruption conditions.

11.2 *Courses attended by department's employees module*

Produce the JSP database navigation structure for a program module which, given a specified department, produces a report listing the following for each employee in the department: employee name, job title and a list of all training courses attended. If a particular employee has not attended any course an appropriate message should be printed. Ignore database corruption conditions.

11.3 *Courses still to be attended module*

(a) Produce the JSP database navigation structure for a program module which, given a specified job title, lists for all employees with that job title all of the courses still to be attended which are required for that job. Ignore database corruption conditions.

(b) Assuming the preliminary program structure has the same structure as the database navigation structure, produce the final program structure with allocated conditions and actions.

12 Beyond testing – optimization

In discussing the qualities of a good program in Chapter 1 the efficiency criterion was briefly aired. In the early days of computers and programming the efficiency of a program was usually very high in the list of anybody's quality criteria of a good program. Those were the days of relatively limited and expensive primary storage, slow CPU processing time and slow peripherals. Times have changed; we now have relatively cheap and fast computer systems, and therefore in many circumstances efficiency criteria take a low priority. However, there are situations in which efficiency has a high priority, in particular in the development of real-time programs and in the development of programs on small and slow microcomputers. The process of improving the efficiency of a program in terms of either increasing execution speed and/or reducing program size is referred to as 'optimization'.

This short chapter concentrates on the small but significant contribution that JSP can make to the optimization of the efficiency of a program.

Optimization and JSP

M. A. Jackson in his book *Principles of Program Design*[1] defines his basic attitude to optimization in two rules:

> *Rule 1:* Don't do it.
> *Rule 2:* Don't do it yet.

Rule 1 *Optimization is not self-justifying*
A positive quantified justification is required before optimization takes place, and often the justification is simply not there. Optimization may result in added costs, namely:

- More time will need to be spent on design and coding.
- More programmer and computer time will be needed for testing.
- There is a greater chance of errors in the program.
- The program is more difficult, time consuming and costly to maintain.

Rule 2 *Optimize a working program only*
No attempt should be made to optimize a program until it has been shown to be working.

A third rule that can be added to Jackson's rule is:

Rule 3 *Do it in stages*
Only one element of a program should be changed at a time. Its effect on the program should be checked to see what improvements have been achieved and what degradation it may have caused in other areas.

If there is justification for optimization it may be in one of two areas: increasing execution speed or reducing program size. In the previous chapter it was pointed out that hierarchic code tends to be the least efficient method of representing a JSP design, particularly as regards execution speed, whereas flat code is the most efficient as regards both execution speed and program size.

The JSP design method tends to produce the fastest possible program, particularly if flat code is used, and hence there is little scope for further improvement in terms of execution speed. The most beneficial way is likely to be by 'tuning', which would have no effect on the design. However, the design technique could be of benefit during tuning, allowing concentration on those parts of the program which correspond to the most frequently executed program components. Tuning is concerned with improvements in the source code (e.g. removal of common subexpressions, replacing divisions by multiplications, choosing efficient data types, efficient use of segmentation), or in the object code (best achieved by the use of an optimizing compiler or similar software), or in the operating environment (e.g. changing blocking factors and/ or number of buffers).

The only change in the design which could potentially affect the execution speed is in the ordering of the child components of a selection component. A selection construct within a program is given in Figure 12.1. If, during the execution of the program, components A, B and C are likely to be executed with equal frequency, then the most efficient ordering, expressed in schematic logic, is that depicted in Figure 12.2, because this will lead to the least number of conditions being tested during the complete execution of the program. If, however, condition C3 occurs 90% of the time and the other conditions with approximately equal frequency, then the most efficient ordering is as depicted in Figure 12.3.

The JSP design method tends also to produce a fairly efficient program in terms of program size, particularly if flat code is used. The greatest improvement in program size is likely to be achieved by the use of optimizing software, e.g. an optimizing compiler, or changes in the operating environment. Changes in the operating environment, such as those already mentioned earlier, usually involve a trade-off between execution speed and program size, i.e. a change may lead to an improvement in one and a degradation in the other.

There are two ways of reducing the size of the source program (and hence the size of the compiled object program), which affect the program design. The first is referred to as 'common action tails' in Michael Jackson's book.[1] Common action tails are sometimes visible in selections and usually less clearly in iterations. An illustration is provided by the selection component expressed in schematic logic in Figure

```
X  sel  if C7
            process component C
X  or   if C5 or C6
            process component B
X  or   if C1 or C2 or C3 or C4
            process component A
X  end
```

Figure 12.2   *Efficient ordering of selection component for equal frequency*

```
X  sel  if C3
            process component A
X  or   if C7
            process component C
X  or   if C5 or C6
            process component B
X  or   if C1 or C2 or C4
            process component A
Z  end
```

Figure 12.3   *Alternative ordering for selection component*

12.4. Action 3 is a common action tail in all three of the selected components, and action 2 in the first and last components. The selection can be coded in optimized COBOL flat code as in Figure 12.5.

You should note that this particular change in the structure of the source code cannot be reflected by a change in the program design, although in other situations this is possible. Hence when making such changes, for the purpose of optimization, the code representing those changes should be clearly marked with comments so that they cannot be mistaken for structure defining statements.

Another example of common action tails is in the iteration of Figure 12.6. Actions 1 and 2 in the iterated component are common with the actions which precede the iteration component. This section of schematic logic can be coded in optimized COBOL flat code as shown in Figure 12.7.

A second method of reducing program size, which is affected by the program design, involves recognizing complete components which are the same or very similar and hiving them off as common subroutines. Where the source code is not exactly the same it is sometimes possible, by introducing new data items and/or switches, to make them the same. Again when making such

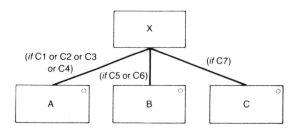

Figure 12.1   *Selection component*

```
X  sel  if C1
            do action 1
            do action 2
            do action 3
X  or   if C2
            do action 4
            do action 5
            do action 3
X  or   do action 6
            do action 2
            do action 3
X  end
```

Figure 12.4 *Common action tails in a selection*

```
X-SEL.
      IF NOT C1 GO TO X-OR1.
      do action 1
CAT-1.
      do action 2
CAT-2.
      do action 3
      GO TO X-END.
X-OR1.
      IF NOT C2 GO TO X-OR2.
      do action 4
      do action 5
      GO TO CAT-2.
                  NOTE. COMMON ACTION TAIL
 .
X-OR2.
      do action 6
      GO TO CAT-1.
                  NOTE. COMMON ACTION TAIL
 .
X-END.
```

Figure 12.5 *COBOL flat code for common action tails in a selection*

```
      do action 1
      do action 2
X iter while C1
            do action 3
            do action 4
            do action 1
            do action 2
X end
```

Figure 12.6 *Common action tail in an iteration*

```
CAT.
      do action 1
      do action 2
X-ITER.
      IF NOT C1 GO TO X-END.
      do action 3
      do action 4
      GO TO CAT.
                  NOTE. COMMON ACTION TAIL.

X-END.
```

Figure 12.7 *COBOL flat code for common action tail in iteration*

changes it is important to clearly mark the code, so that the use of common subroutines for optimization purposes is clear. Before concluding this chapter it is worth mentioning that the software package JSP-COBOL, described in Chapter 7, optimizes the generated source code to make the object code more efficient.

Exercises

12.1 Update stock master program (second version).
For the detailed design produced for Exercise 6.3, identify possible optimizations of the implemented program:
(a) if 1 per cent of the movement records are likely to have non-matching master records and the hit rate of the other movement records is likely to be about 20 per cent;
(b) by recognizing complete components which are the same or very similar and hiving them off as common subroutines;
(c) by finding common action tails.

References

1 M. A. Jackson, *Principles of Program Design* (Academic Press, 1985).
2 L. Ingevaldsson, *JSP – A Practical Method of Program Design* (Input Two-Nine, 1979).
3 J. Triance, *Structured COBOL Programming* (NCC Publications, 1983).
4 Michael Jackson Systems Ltd, *JSP-COBOL Sampler Manual* (Michael Jackson Systems Ltd, 1979).
5 J. M. Triance and J. F. S. Yow, 'Experiences with a schematic logic preprocessor', *Software Practice and Experience*, **10**, October 1980.
6 G. J. Myers, *The Art of Software Testing* (Wiley Interscience, 1979).
7 Civil Service Department, Central Computer Agency guide no. 9, *Program Validation* (HMSO).
8 J. R. Cameron, *JSP & JSD: The Jackson Approach to Software Development* (IEEE Computer Society Press, 1983).
9 A. Cohen, *Structure Logic and Program Design* (Wiley, 1983).
10 R. S. Burgess, *Introduction to Program Design Using JSP* (Hutchinson, 1984).
11 M. J. King and J. P. Pardoe, *Program Design Using JSP* (Macmillan, 1985).

Solutions to exercises

Some of the solutions presented are based upon solutions to examples or exercises presented earlier in the text.

2.1 (a) *Sequence components*

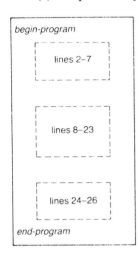

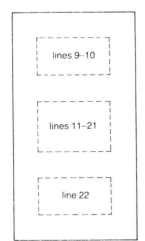

Iteration components

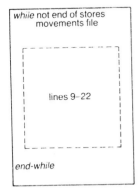

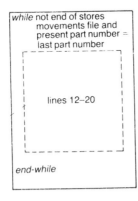

Selection component

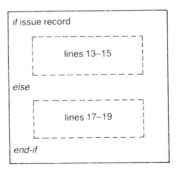

Elementary components
Lines 2–7, lines 9–10, lines 13–15, lines 17–19, line 22 and lines 24–26.

(b) *Actions list*
1 Open stores movements file.
2 Open movements analysis report.
3 Print report headings.
4 Zeroize issues total.
5 Zeroize receipts total.
6 Read first part movement record.
7 Zeroize part net movement total.
8 Store part number of present movement record in last part number.
9 Increase issues total by 1.
10 Subtract quantity issued from part net movement total.
11 Read next part movement record.
12 Increase receipts total by 1.
13 Add quantity received to part net movement total.
14 Print part number report line.
15 Print summary line.
16 Close stores movements file.
17 Close movements analysis report.

(c) *Conditions list*
C1 End of stores movements file?
C2 Present part number = last part number?
C3 Issue record?

(d)   *Data characteristics reflected in program*

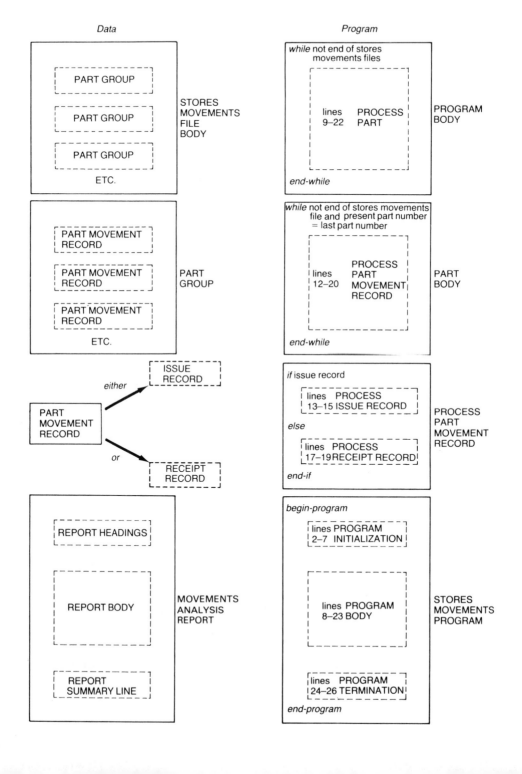

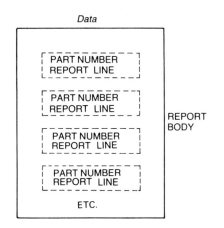

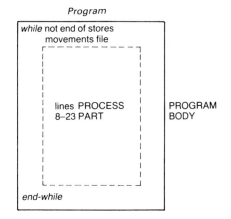

(e) *JSP program structure diagram*

3.1

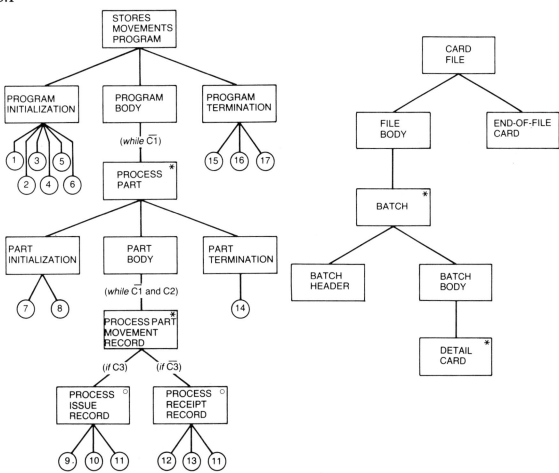

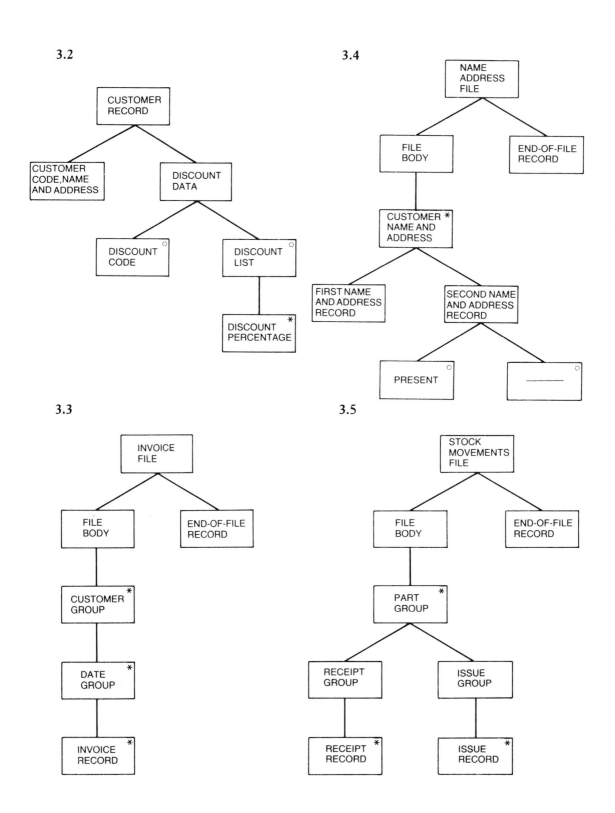

3.6 (a)

3.7 (a)

(b)

(b)

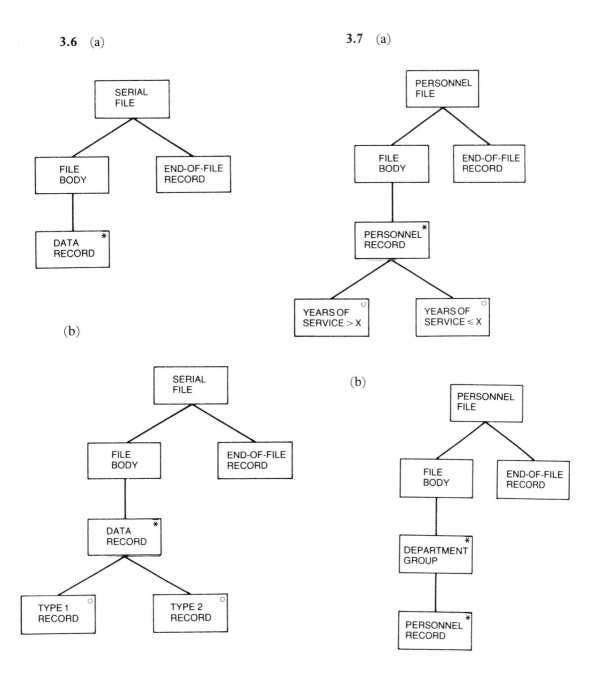

(c)

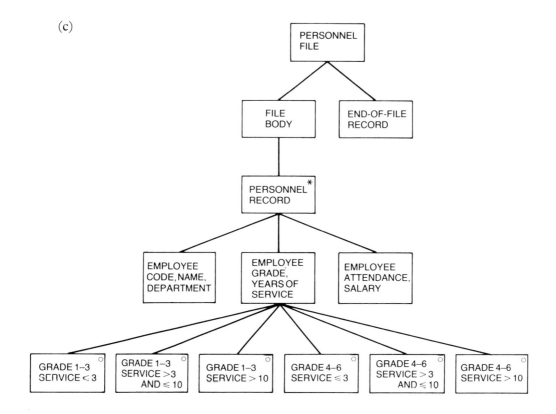

3.8

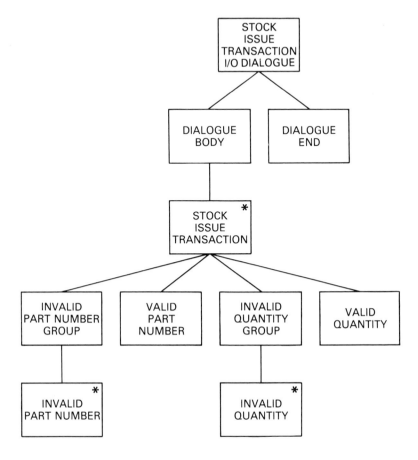

4.1 Job costing program (first version)

(a) *Correspondences*

Job costing file component	*Job costs summary report component*
1	1
–	2
2	3
3	4
4	5
6	–
7	–
8	–
9	–
10	–
11	–

(b)   *Matched data structures*

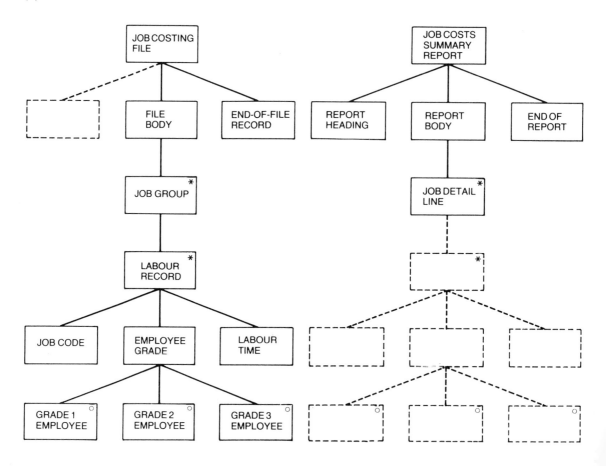

(c) *Preliminary program structure*

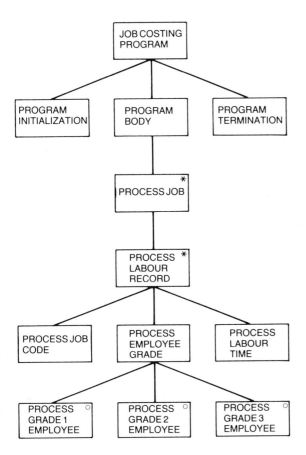

4.2   Employees holiday program
    (a)   *Personnel file data structure*

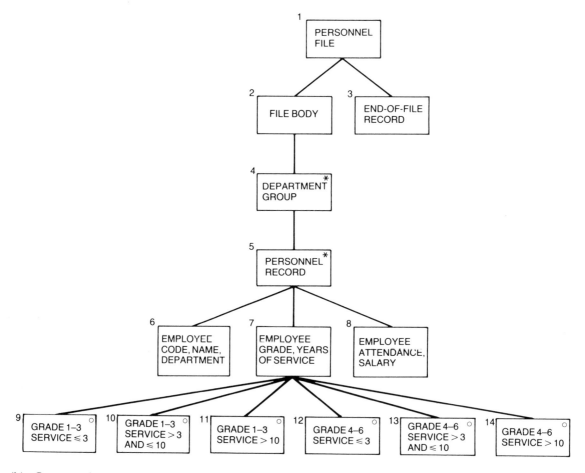

(b)   *Correspondences*

Personnel file component	Employee holidays report component
1	1
2	–
3	–
4	2
–	3
–	4
5	5
6, 7, 8, 9, 10, 11, 12, 13, 14	–

(c) *Matched data structures*

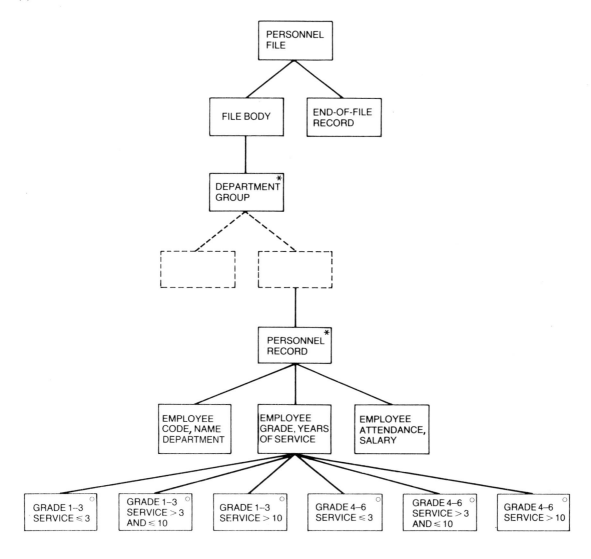

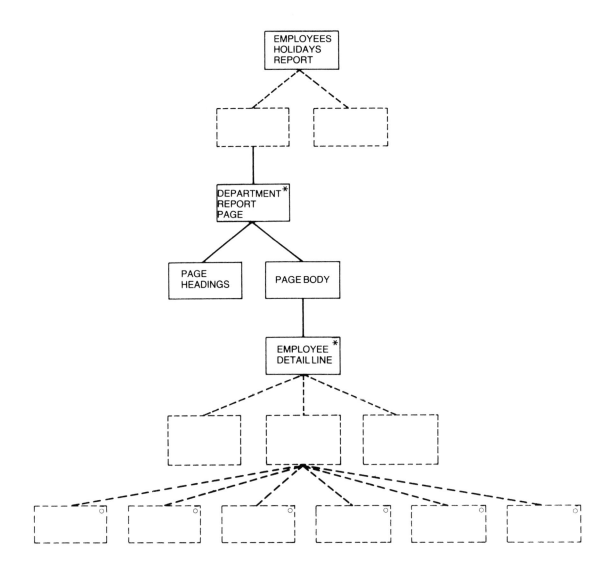

(d) *Preliminary program structure*

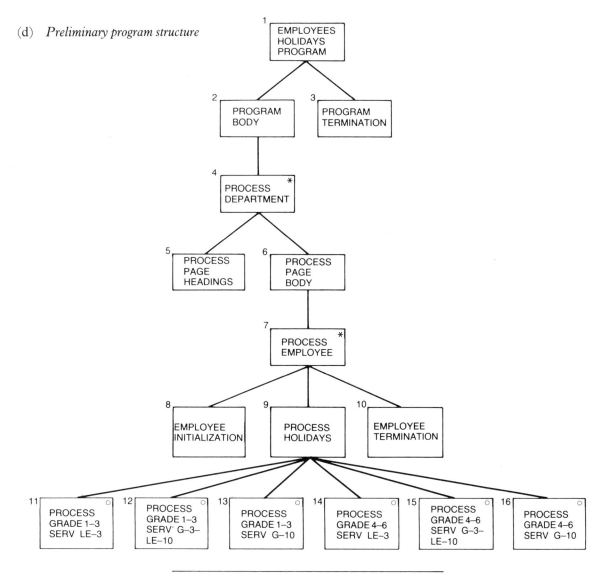

Component no.	Comment
11	Process employee with grade 1–3, service ≤ 3
12	Process employee with grade 1–3, service > 3 and ≤ 10
13	Process employee with grade 1–3, service > 10
14	Process employee with grade 4–6, service ≤ 3
15	Process employee with grade 4–6, service > 3 and ≤ 10
16	Process employee with grade 4–6, service > 10

(e)   *The impact on the employees holidays report data structure*

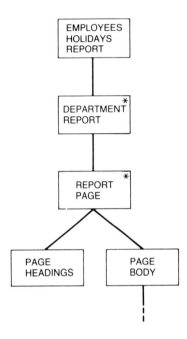

It is left to the reader to assess the impact of this changed data structure on the preliminary program structure.

4.3   Job costing program (second version)
(a)   *Data structures*

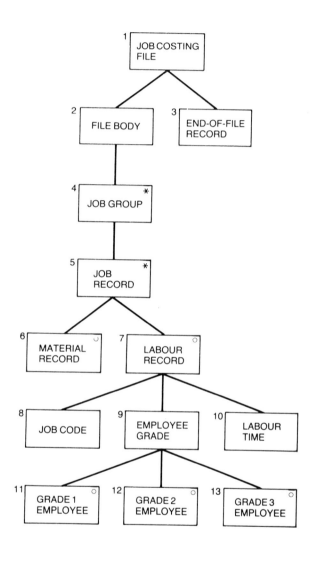

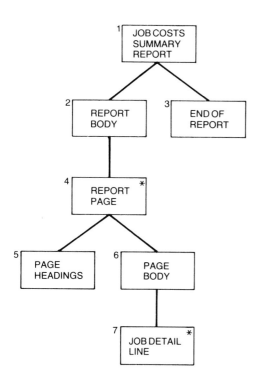

(b) *Correspondences*

Job costing file component	Job costs summary report component
1	1
2	2
3	3
–	4
–	5
–	6
4	7
5, 6, 7, 8, 9, 10, 11, 12, 13	–

(c) *Matched data structures*

(d) *Preliminary program structure*

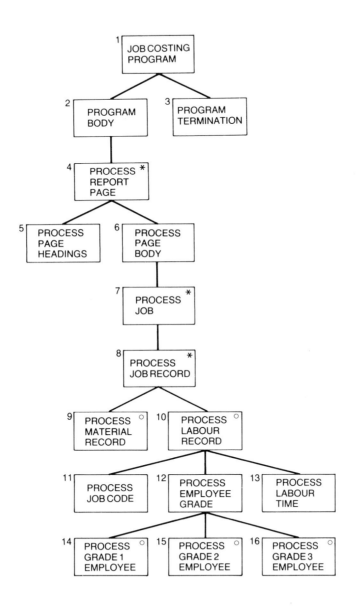

4.4   Stock status program
(a)   *Data structures*

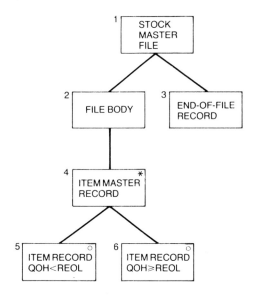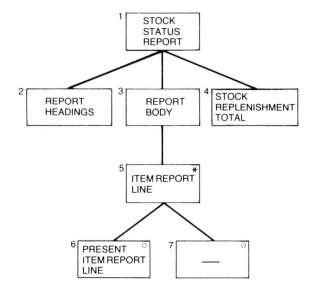

(b)   *Correspondences*

Stock master file component	Stock status report component
1	1
–	2
2	3
3	4
4	5
5	6
6	7

(c) *Matched data structures*

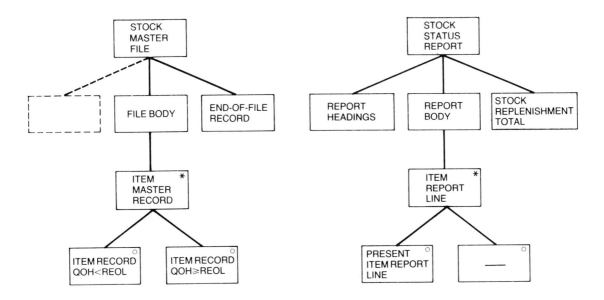

(d) *Preliminary program structure*

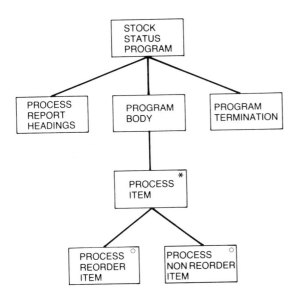

4.5   Demerge file program
(a)   *Data structures*

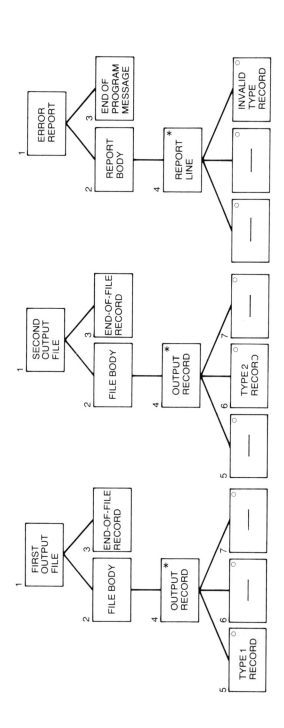

(b) *Correspondences*
All components correspond according to physical position.
(c) *Matched data structures*
The data structures are matched without any further manipulation of the structures.
(d) *Preliminary program structure*
See Figure 2.14.

5.1   Job costing program (third version)
(a)   *Data structures*

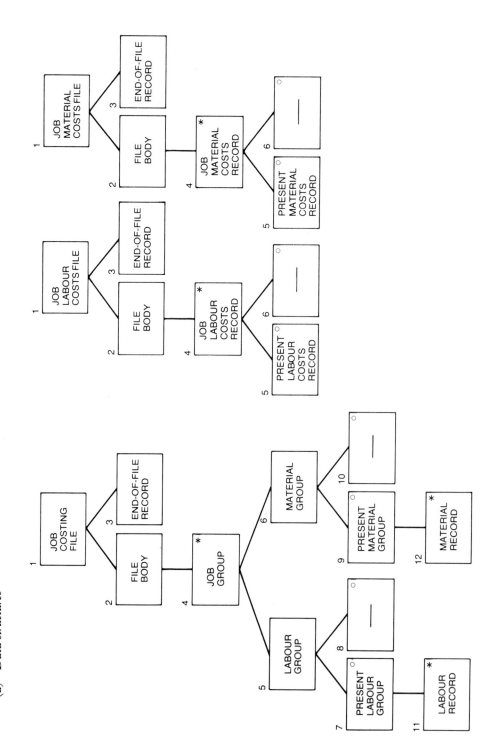

(b) *Correspondences*

Job costing file component	Job labour costs file component	Job material costs file component
1	1	1
2	2	2
3	3	3
4	4	4
5	–	–
6	–	–
7	5	–
8	6	–
9	–	5
10	–	6
11	–	–
12	–	–

(c) *Matched data structures*

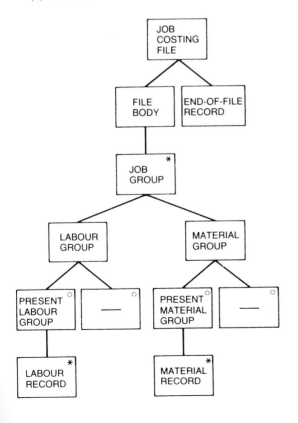
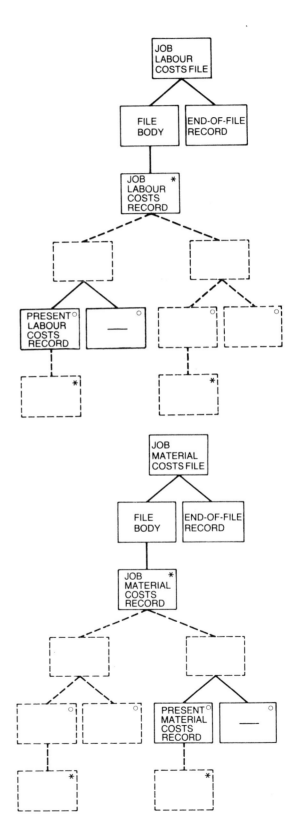

(d) *Preliminary program structure*

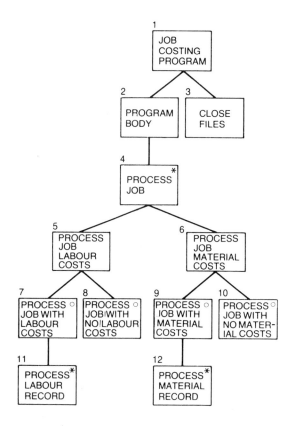

5.2 Update stock master program (first version)

(a) *Data structures*

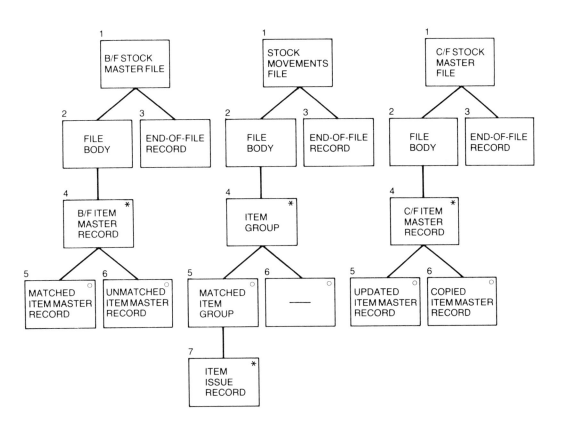

(b) *Correspondences*

B/F stock master file component	Stock movements file component	C/F stock master file component
1	1	1
2	2	2
3	3	3
4	4	4
5	5	5
6	6	6
–	7	–

(c) *Matched data structures*
Achieved by adding dummy iterated
component to component 5 in both master
file data structures:

(d) *Preliminary program structure*

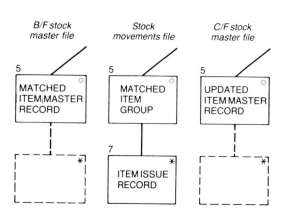

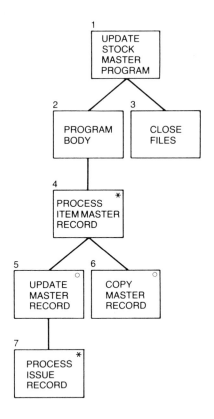

5.3   Update stock master program (second
version)
(a)   *Data structures*

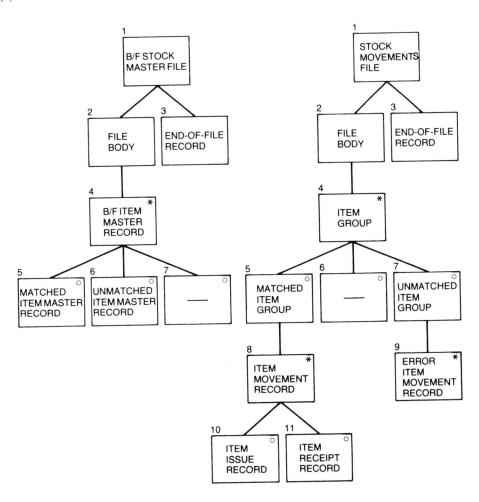

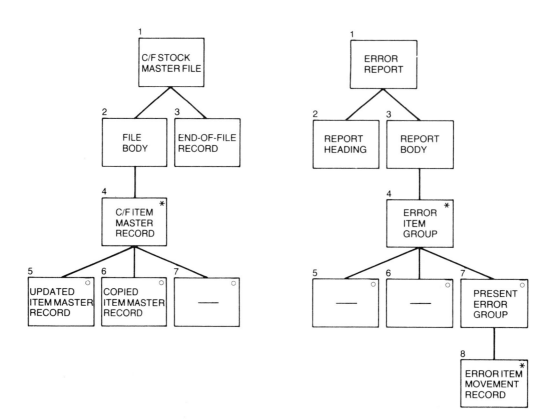

(b) *Correspondences*

B/F stock master file component	*Stock movements file component*	*C/F stock master file component*	*Error report component*
1	1	1	1
–	–	–	2
2	2	2	3
3	3	3	–
4	4	4	4
5	5	5	5
6	6	6	6
7	7	7	7
–	8	–	–
–	9	–	8
–	10	–	–
–	11		

(c) *Matched data structures*

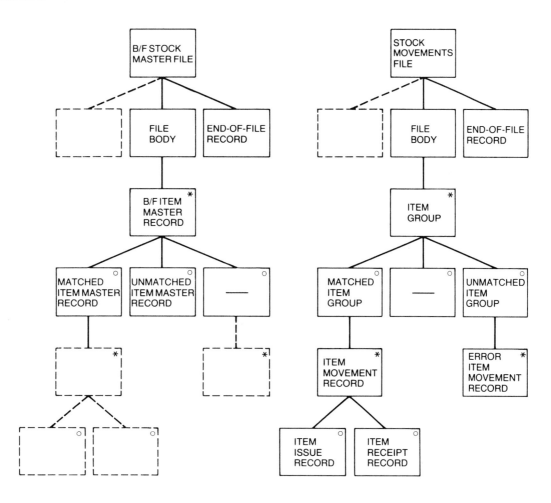

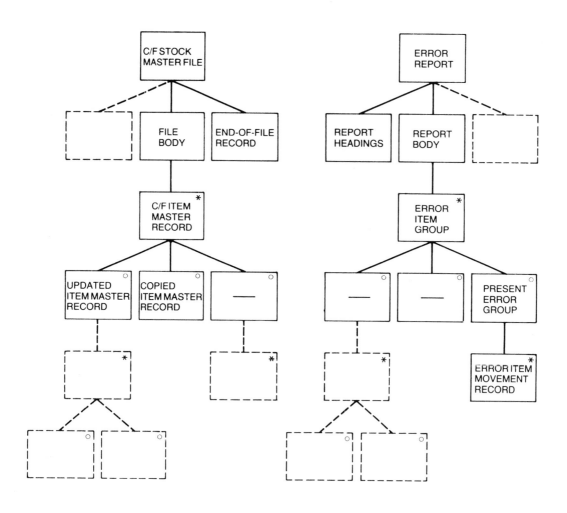

(d) *Preliminary program structure*

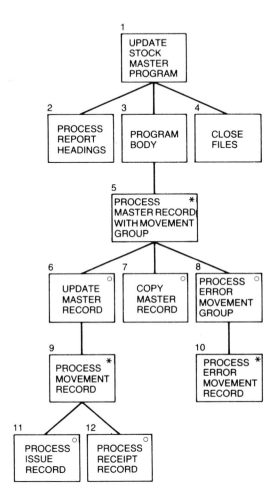

5.4   IS stock amendments program
   (a)   *Data structures*

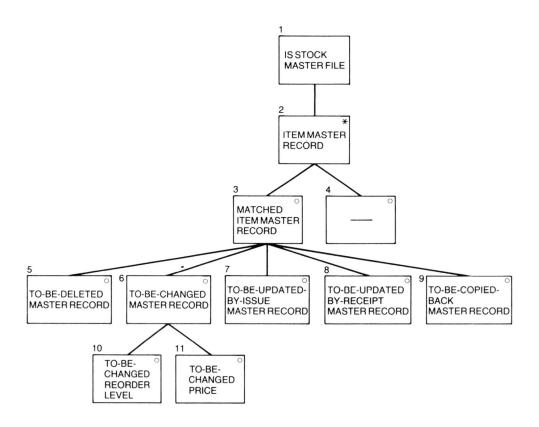

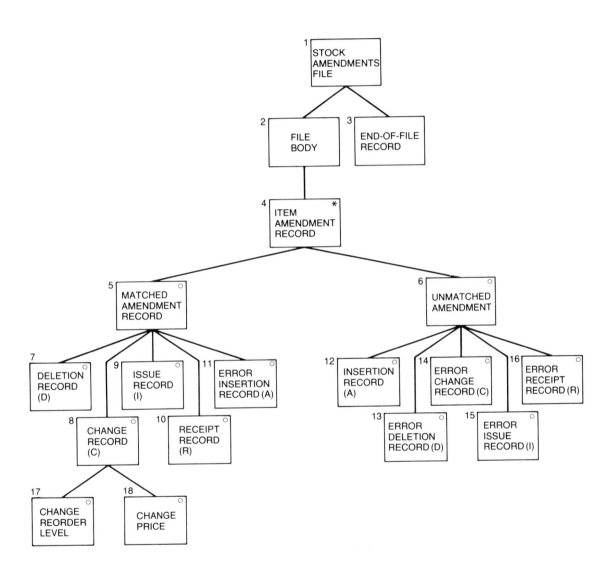

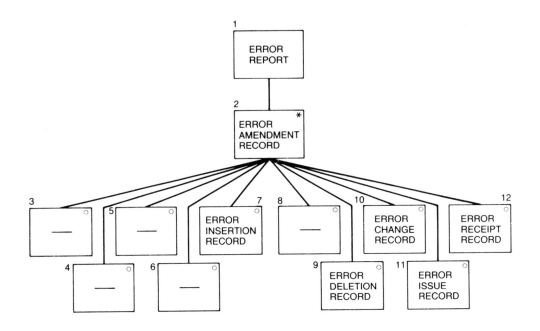

(b)   *Correspondences*

IS stock master file component	Stock amendments file component	Error report components
1	1	1
–	2	–
–	3	–
2	4	2
3	5	–
4	6	–
5	7	3
6	8	4
7	9	5
8	10	6
9	11	7
–	12	8
–	13	9
–	14	10
–	15	11
–	16	12
10	17	–
11	18	–

(c) *Matched data structures (see also p. 194)*

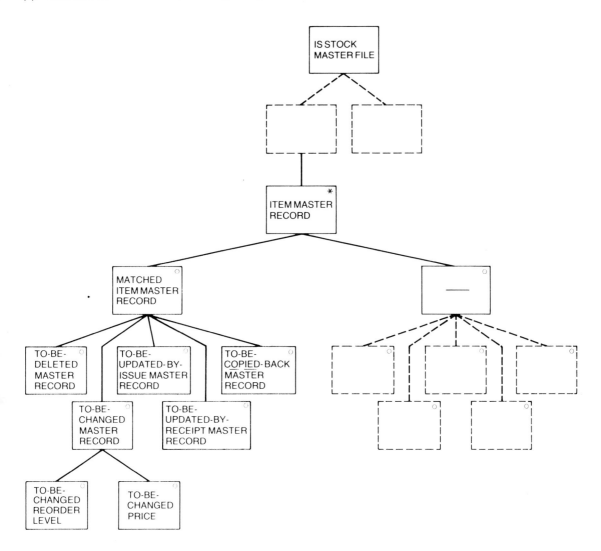

Stock amendments file is unchanged from
data structure presented in (a).

(c) *Matched data structures (cont.)*

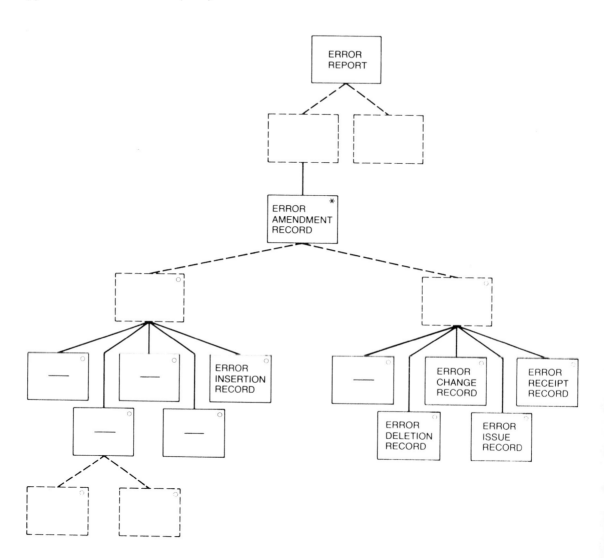

(d) *Preliminary program structure*

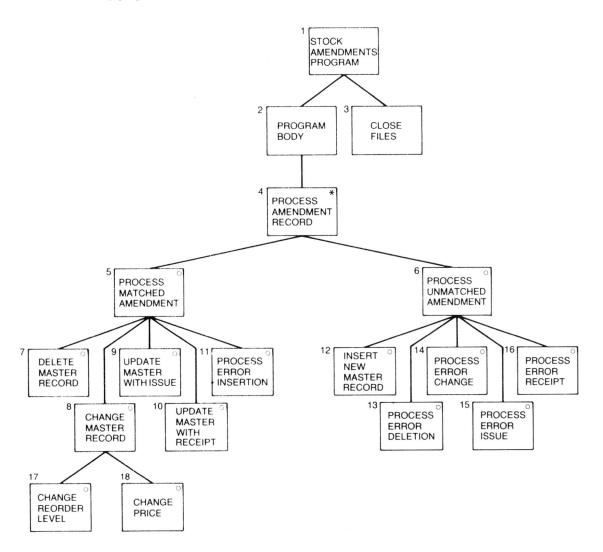

6.1   Employees holidays program

(a)   *Conditions list*

C1	End of personnel file?
C2	Present department code = previous department code?
C3	Employee grade ≥ 1?
C4	Employee grade ≤ 3?
C5	Employee grade ≤ 6?
C6	Employee service ≤ 3?
C7	Employee service ≤ 10?

(b)   *Actions list*

1	Stop program.
2	Open personnel file.
3	Open employees holidays report.
4	Close personnel file.
5	Close employees holidays report.
6	Read first personnel record.
7	Read next personnel record.
8	Store department code in page headings.
9	Print page headings.
10	Store employee code in employee detail line.
11	Store employee name in employee detail line.
12	Store 15 in number of days of holiday for employee detail line.
13	Store 20 in number of days of holiday for employee detail line.
14	Store 25 in number of days of holiday for employee detail line.
15	Store 30 in number of days of holiday for employee detail line.
16	Print employee detail line.
17	Store present department code in previous department code.

This is not necessarily an exhaustive list of actions; further actions may be needed depending on the design of the error report. For instance, if each page is numbered then the following actions are required:

18	Zeroize page count.
19	Increase page count by 1.
20	Store page count in page headings.

It is left to the reader to allocate these possible additional actions to the program structure.

(c) *Final program structure with allocated
actions and conditions*

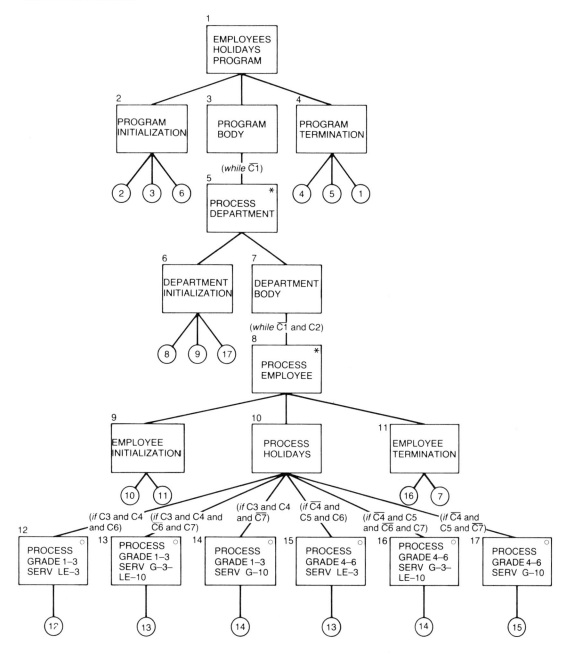

6.2   Job costing program (second version)
   (a)   *Conditions list*
      C1   End of job costing file?
      C2   End of page?
      C2   Present job code = previous job code?
      C4   Labour record?
      C5   Material record?
      C6   Grade 1 employee?
      C7   Grade 2 employee?
      C8   Grade 3 employee?

   (b)   *Actions list*
      1   Stop program.
      2   Open job costing file.
      3   Open job cost summary report.
      4   Close job costing file.
      5   Close job cost summary report.
      6   Read first job costing record.
      7   Read next job costing record.
      8   Print page headings.
      9   Rate of pay = 4.70.
      10   Rate of pay = 4.00.
      11   Rate of pay = 3.10.
      12   Calculate employee labour cost = rate of pay × labour time.
      13   Add employee labour cost to job labour cost.
      14   Zeroize job labour cost.
      15   Calculate overheads cost = 5.00 × labour time.
      16   Add overheads cost to job overheads cost.
      17   Zeroize job overheads cost.
      18   Add material cost to job material costs.
      19   Zeroize job material costs.
      20   Set up job detail line.
      21   Print job detail line.
      22   Store present job code in previous job code.

Further actions may be required relating to the job costing summary report. For example, if the 'end of page?' condition is detected by counting the number of job detail lines printed and comparing the count to the maximum number of job detail lines that can be printed on one page, then the following actions are required:

   23   Zeroize line count.
   24   Increase line count by 1.

Furthermore, if each page of the job cost summary report contains a page number then the following actions are required:

   25   Zeroize page count.
   26   Increase page count by 1.
   27   Store page count in page headings.

(c) *Final program structure with allocated actions and conditions*

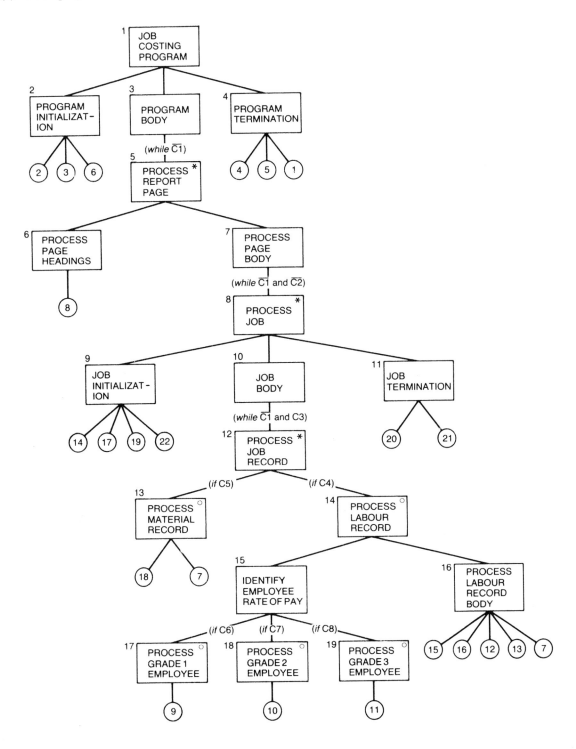

6.3   Update stock master program (second version)

(a)   *Conditons list*

C1   End of stock movements file?
C2   End of B/F stock master file?
C3   Movement key = master key?
C4   Movement key < master key?
C5   Movement key > master key?
C6   Present movement key = previous movement key?
C7   Issue record?
C8   Receipt record?

(b)   *Actions list*

1   Stop program.
2   Open stock movements file.
3   Open B/F stock master file.
4   Open C/F stock master file.
5   Open error report.
6   Close stock movements file.
7   Close B/F stock master file.
8   Close C/F stock master file.
9   Close error report.
10   Read first movement record.
11   Read next movement record.
12   Read first B/F master record.
13   Read next B/F master record.
14   Print report headings.
15   Copy movement record to error movement record.
16   Copy B/F master record to C/F master record.
17   Print error movement record.
18   Write C/F master record.
19   Subtract quantity issued from quantity on hand.
20   Add quantity received to quantity on hand.
21   Store movement key in previous movement key.

(c) *Final program structure with allocated conditions and actions*

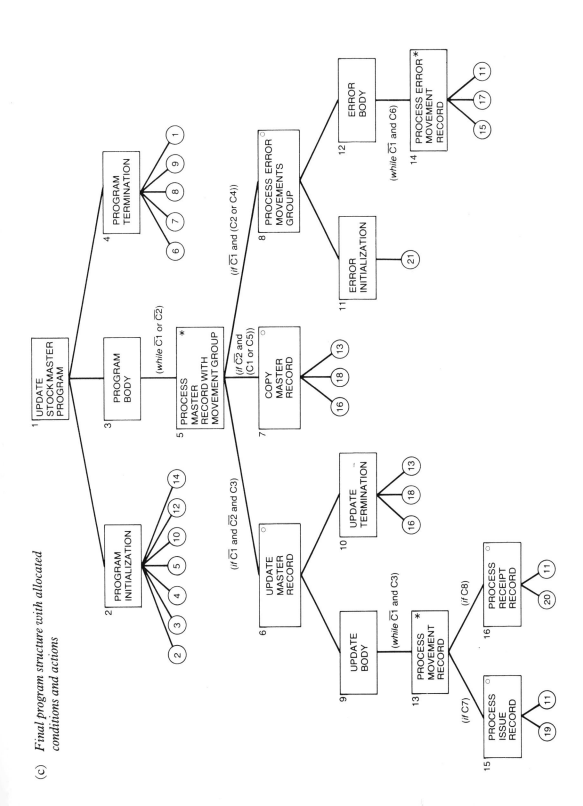

6.4   IS stock amendments program
  (a)   *Conditions list*
       C1   End of amendments file?
       C2   Master record present?
       C3   Record type = A?
       C4   Record type = D?
       C5   Record type = C?
       C6   Record type = I?
       C7   Record type = R?
       C8   Change type code = 1?
       C9   Change type code = 2?

  (b)   *Actions list*
       1   Stop program
       2   Open stock amendments file.
       3   Open stock master file.
       4   Open error report.
       5   Close stock amendments file.
       6   Close stock master file.
       7   Close error report.
       8   Read first amendment record.
       9   Read next amendment record.
       10   Read master record with specified master key.
       11   Store amendment key in master key.
       12   Rewrite master record.
       13   Move amendment record to error amendment record.
       14   Print error amendment record.
       15   Store amendment reorder level in master reorder level.
       16   Store amendment price in master record price.
       17   Subtract quantity issued from quantity on hand.
       18   Add quantity received to quantity on hand.
       19   Move amendment record to master record.
       20   Write master record.

(c) *Program structure with allocated*
    conditions and actions

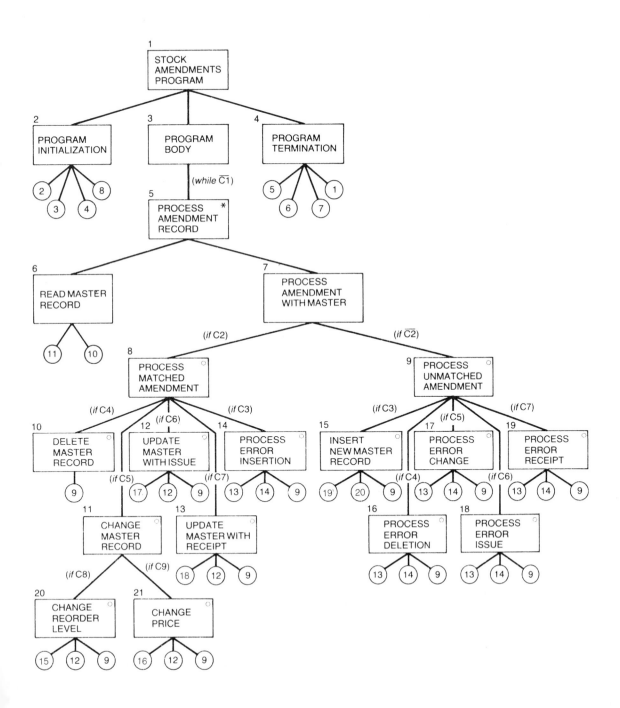

7.1

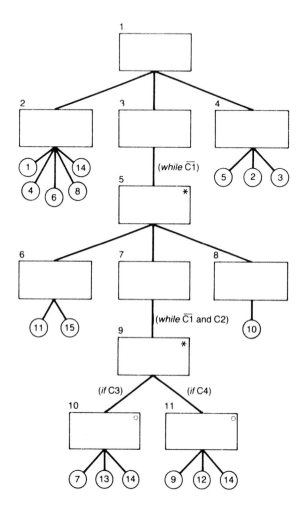

7.2

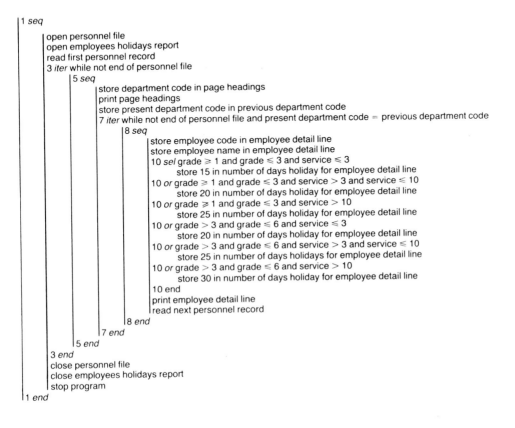

```
1 seq
    open personnel file
    open employees holidays report
    read first personnel record
    3 iter while not end of personnel file
        5 seq
            store department code in page headings
            print page headings
            store present department code in previous department code
            7 iter while not end of personnel file and present department code = previous department code
                8 seq
                    store employee code in employee detail line
                    store employee name in employee detail line
                    10 sel grade ≥ 1 and grade ≤ 3 and service ≤ 3
                        store 15 in number of days holiday for employee detail line
                    10 or grade ≥ 1 and grade ≤ 3 and service > 3 and service ≤ 10
                        store 20 in number of days holiday for employee detail line
                    10 or grade ≥ 1 and grade ≤ 3 and service > 10
                        store 25 in number of days holiday for employee detail line
                    10 or grade > 3 and grade ≤ 6 and service ≤ 3
                        store 20 in number of days holiday for employee detail line
                    10 or grade > 3 and grade ≤ 6 and service > 3 and service ≤ 10
                        store 25 in number of days holidays for employee detail line
                    10 or grade > 3 and grade ≤ 6 and service > 10
                        store 30 in number of days holiday for employee detail line
                    10 end
                    print employee detail line
                    read next personnel record
                8 end
            7 end
        5 end
    3 end
    close personnel file
    close employees holidays report
    stop program
1 end
```

8.1 (a) and (b) *Data structures and correspondences*

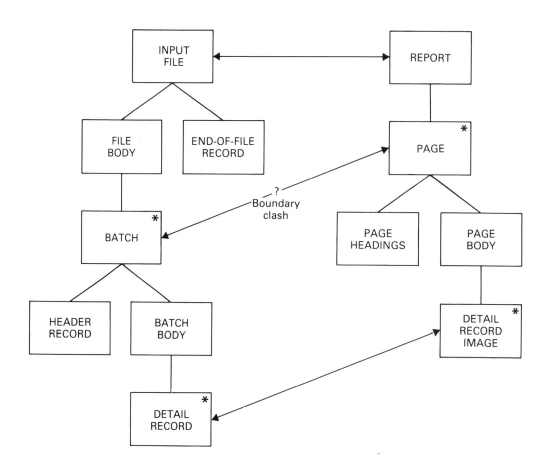

(c) *Schematic logic for two programs using intermediate file*

```
INPUT-PROGRAM seq
    open input-file
    open intermediate-file
    read input-record
    PROGRAM-BODY iter while not end-of-input-file
        copy batch-number to previous-batch-number
        PROCESS-BATCH seq
            read input-record
            PROCESS-BATCH-BODY iter while not end-of-input-file
                    and batch-number = previous-batch-number
                write detail-record to intermediate-file
                read input-record
            PROCESS-BATCH-BODY end
        PROCESS-BATCH end
    PROGRAM-BODY end
    close input-file
    close intermediate-file
    stop program
INPUT-PROGRAM end

REPORT-PROGRAM seq
    open intermediate-file
    open report
    read intermediate-record
    PROCESS-PAGE iter while not end-of-intermediate-file
        print page-headings
        PROCESS-PAGE-BODY iter while not end-of-intermediate-file
                            and not full-page
            print intermediate-record on report
            read intermediate-record
        PROCESS-PAGE-BODY end
    PROCESS-PAGE end
    close-intermediate-file
    close report
    stop run
REPORT-PROGRAM end
```

(d) *Schematic logic when using program inversion*

```
INPUT-PROGRAM seq
    open input-file
    set intermediate-file-switch to zero
    read input-record
    PROGRAM-BODY iter while not end-of-input-file
        copy batch-number to previous-batch-number
        PROCESS-BATCH seq
            read input-record
            PROCESS-BATCH-BODY iter while not end-of-input-file
                    and batch-number = previous-batch-number
                call REPORT-SUBROUTINE
                    using input-record, intermediate-file-switch
                read input-record
            PROCESS-BATCH-BODY end
        PROCESS-BATCH end
    PROGRAM-BODY end
    close input-file
    set intermediate-file-switch to 1
    call REPORT-SUBROUTINE
        using null-intermediate-file-record, intermediate-file-switch
    stop program
INPUT-PROGRAM end

REPORT-SUBROUTINE seq
    go to READ-FIRST-INT-RECORD
            READ-NEXT-INT-RECORD
        depending on entry-status
READ-FIRST-INT-RECORD.
    open report
    PROCESS-PAGE iter while intermediate-file-switch = 0
        print page-headings
        PROCESS-PAGE-BODY iter while intermediate-file-switch = 0
                            and not full-page
            print intermediate-record on report
            set entry-status to 2
            exit subroutine
READ-NEXT-INT-RECORD.
        PROCESS-PAGE-BODY end
    PROCESS-PAGE end
    close report
    exit subroutine
REPORT-SUBROUTINE end
```

9.1   *Name and address program*

(a)   *Schematic logic after standard JSP method applied*

```
1-PROGRAM seq
    open name and address file
    open print file
    read name and address record
    3-PROGRAM-BODY iter while not end of name and address file
        5-PR-NAME-AND-ADD sel if five line name and address
            copy name and address record to print line
            read name and address record
            copy name and address record to print line
            read name and address record
            copy name and address record to print line
            write print line
            read name and address record
            copy name and address record to print line
            read name and address record
            copy name and address record to print line
            write print line
            read name and address record
        5-PR-NAME-AND-ADD or if four line name and address
            copy name and address record to print line
            read name and address record
            copy name and address record to print line
            write print line
            read name and address record
            copy name and address record to print line
            read name and address record
            copy name and address record to print line
            write print line
            read name and address record
        5-PR-NAME-AND-ADD end
    3-PROGRAM-BODY end
    close print file
    close name and address file
    stop program
1-PROGRAM end
```

(b)   *Schematic logic using multiple read ahead*

```
1-PROGRAM seq
    open name and address file
    open print file
    zeroize name and address line count
    read name and address record
    6-READ-FIRST-NA iter while same customer code and not end of
                                        name and address file
        add 1 to name and address line count
        copy name and address record
            to name and address table (name and address line count)
        read name and address record
    6-READ-FIRST-NA end
    3-PROGRAM-BODY iter while name and address line count not = 0
        7-PR-NAME-AND-ADD sel if name and address line count = 5
            copy name and address table (1) to print line
            copy name and address table (2) to print line
            copy name and address table (3) to print line
            write print line
            copy name and address table (4) to print line
            copy name and address table (5) to print line
            write print line
            zeroize name and address line count
            12-READ-NEXT-NA iter while same customer code
                            and not end of name and address file
                add 1 to name and address line count
                copy name and address record
                    to name and address table (name and address line co■
                read name and address record
            12-READ-NEXT-NA end
        7-PR-NAME-AND-ADD or if name and address line count = 4
            copy name and address table (1) to print line
            copy name and address table (2) to print line
            write print line
            copy name and address table (3) to print line
            copy name and address table (4) to print line
            write print line
            zeroize name and address line count
            14-READ-NEXT-NA iter while same customer code
                            and not end of name and address file
                add 1 to name and address line count
                copy name and address record
                    to name and address table (name and
                                    address line count)
                read name and address record
            14-READ-NEXT-NA end
        7-PR-NAME-AND-ADD end
    3-PROGRAM-BODY end
    close print file
    close name and address file
    stop program
1-PROGRAM end
```

(c)   *Schematic logic using backtracking*

```
1-PROGRAM seq
    open name and address file
    open print file
    read name and address record
    3-PROGRAM-BODY iter while not end of name and address file
        5-PR-NAME-AND-ADD posit five line name and address
            copy name and address record to name and address table (1)
            read name and address record
            copy name and address record to name and address table (2)
            read name and address record
            copy name and address record to name and address table (3)
            read name and address record
            copy name and address record to name and address table (4)
            read name and address record
            quit posit if not same customer code or end of name and address file
            copy name and address table (1) to print line
            copy name and address table (2) to print line
            copy name and address table (3) to print line
            write print line
            copy name and address table (4) to print line
            copy name and address record to print line
            write print line
            read name and address record
        5-PR-NAME-AND-ADD admit four line name and address
            copy name and address table (1) to print line
            copy name and address table (2) to print line
            write print line
            copy name and address table (3) to print line
            copy name and address table (4) to print line
            write print line
        5-PR-NAME-AND-ADD end
    3-PROGRAM-BODY end
    close print file
    close name and address file
    stop program
1-PROGRAM end
```

9.2   *Batches program*

(a)   *Schematic logic before backtracking applied*

```
1-PROGRAM seq
    open input file
    open output file
    read first batch header record
    3-PROGRAM-BODY iter while not end of input file
        5-PROCESS-BATCH seq
            zeroize no of detail records count
            read first detail record of batch
            7-PR-BATCH-BODY sel if good batch
                8-PR-GOOD-BATCH iter while not end of input file
                                    and not change of batch
                    add 1 to no of detail records count
                    copy detail record to output record
                    write output record
                    read next input record
                8-PR-GOOD BATCH end
            7-PR-BATCH-BODY or if bad batch
                9-PR-BAD-BATCH iter while not end of input file
                                    and not change of batch
                    read next input record
                9-PR-BAD-BATCH end
            7-PR-BATCH-BODY end
        5-PROCESS-BATCH end
    3-PROGRAM-BODY end
    close input file
    close output file
1-PROGRAM end
```

(b) *Schematic logic after backtracking applied*

```
1-PROGRAM seq
    open input file
    open output file
    read first batch header record
    3-PROGRAM-BODY iter while not end of input file
        5-PROCESS-BATCH seq
            zeroize no of detail records count
            read first detail record of batch
            7-PR-BATCH-BODY posit good batch
                8-PR-GOOD-BATCH seq
                    open work file
                    11-STORE-WORK-BATCH iter while not end of input file
                                                and not change of batch
                        add 1 to no of detail records count
                        copy detail record to work record
                        write work record
                        read next input record
                    11-STORE-WORK-BATCH end
                    close work file
                    quit posit if no detail records count not =
                                            batch header total
                    open work file
                    read first work record
                    13-WRITE-WORK-BATCH iter while not end of work file
                        copy work record to output record
                        write output record
                        read next work record
                    13-WRITE-WORK-BATCH end
                    close work file
                8-PR-GOOD-BATCH end
            7-PR-BATCH-BODY admit bad batch
                (do nothing)
            7-PR-BATCH-BODY end
        5-PROCESS-BATCH end
    3-PROGRAM-BODY end
    close input file
    close output file
1-PROGRAM end
```

9.3 *Month conversion subroutine*

(a) *Schematic logic before backtracking applied*

```
1-SUBROUTINE seq
    initialize subscript to 1
    3-SEARCH-TABLE iter while month in table and not yet found
        5-INSPECT-TABLE-ENTRY sel if month-name = month-table (subscript)
            copy subscript to month-number
        5-INSPECT-TABLE-ENTRY or if month-name not = month-table (subscript)
                                    and subscript < 12
            add 1 to subscript
        5-INSPECT-TABLE-ENTRY or if month-name not = month-table (subscript)
                                    and subscript = 12
            copy zero to month-number
        5-INSPECT-TABLE-ENTRY end
    3-SEARCH-TABLE end
    exit subroutine
1-SUBROUTINE end
```

(b)   *Schematic logic after backtracking applied*

```
1-SUBROUTINE seq
    initialize subscript to 1
    3-SEARCH-TABLE iter month in table and not yet found
        5-INSPECT-TABLE-ENTRY sel if month-name = month-table (subscript)
            copy subscript to month-number
            quit 3-SEARCH-TABLE iter
        5-INSPECT-TABLE-ENTRY or if month-name not = month-table (subscript)
                                   and subscript < 12
            add 1 to subscript
        5-INSPECT-TABLE-ENTRY or if month-name not = month-table (subscript)
                                   and subscript = 12
            copy zero to month-number
            quit 3-SEARCH-TABLE iter
        5-INSPECT-TABLE-ENTRY end
    3-SEARCH-TABLE end
    exit subroutine
1-SUBROUTINE end
```

(*Note.* The *quit* actions are conditionless in this solution and therefore effectively equate to an unconditional transfer of control.)

10.1   (a)   *Flowschema*

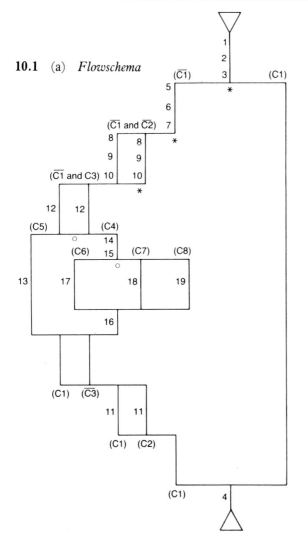

(b) *Test paths*

Test path no.	Path conditions
1	$\overline{C1}$, $\overline{C1}$ and $\overline{C2}$, $\overline{C1}$ and C3, C5, (C1), (C1), (C1)
2	$\overline{C1}$, $\overline{C1}$ and $\overline{C2}$, $\overline{C1}$ and C3, C5, (C1), (C2), (C1)
3	$\overline{C1}$, $\overline{C1}$ and C2, $\overline{C1}$ and C3, C5, $(\overline{C3})$, (C1), (C1)
4	$\overline{C1}$, $\overline{C1}$ and C2, $\overline{C1}$ and C3, C5, $(\overline{C3})$, (C2), (C1)
5	$\overline{C1}$, $\overline{C1}$ and $\overline{C2}$, $\overline{C1}$ and C3, C4, C6, (C1), (C1), (C1)
6	$\overline{C1}$, $\overline{C1}$ and $\overline{C2}$, $\overline{C1}$ and C3, C4, C6, $(\overline{C3})$, (C1), (C1)
7	$\overline{C1}$, $\overline{C1}$ and $\overline{C2}$, $\overline{C1}$ and C3, C4, C6, $(\overline{C3})$, (C2), (C1)
8	$\overline{C1}$, $\overline{C1}$ and $\overline{C2}$, $\overline{C1}$ and C3, C4, C7, (C1), (C1), (C1)
9	$\overline{C1}$, $\overline{C1}$ and $\overline{C2}$, $\overline{C1}$ and C3, C4, C7, $(\overline{C3})$, (C1), (C1)
10	$\overline{C1}$, $\overline{C1}$ and $\overline{C2}$, $\overline{C1}$ and C3, C4, C7, $(\overline{C3})$, (C2), (C1)
11	$\overline{C1}$, $\overline{C1}$ and $\overline{C2}$, $\overline{C1}$ and C3, C4, C8, (C1), (C1), (C1)
12	$\overline{C1}$, $\overline{C1}$ and $\overline{C2}$, $\overline{C1}$ and C3, C4, C8, $(\overline{C3})$, (C1), (C1)
13	$\overline{C1}$, $\overline{C1}$ and $\overline{C2}$, $\overline{C1}$ and C3, C4, C8, $(\overline{C3})$, (C2), (C1)
14	C1

(c) *Test data*

Test path no.	Test data
1	One material record, followed by end-of-file record
2	Impossible path
3	Two material records for same job, followed by end-of-file record
4	Material records for enough jobs to fill more than one page, followed by end-of-file record
5, 6, 7	Same as for 1, 3 and 4 except with labour records with employee grade = 1
8, 9, 10	Same as for 5, 6 and 7 except with labour records with employee grade = 2
11, 12, 13	Same as for 5, 6 and 7 except with labour records with employee grade = 3
14	End-of-file record

10.2   (a)   *Flowschema for batches program*

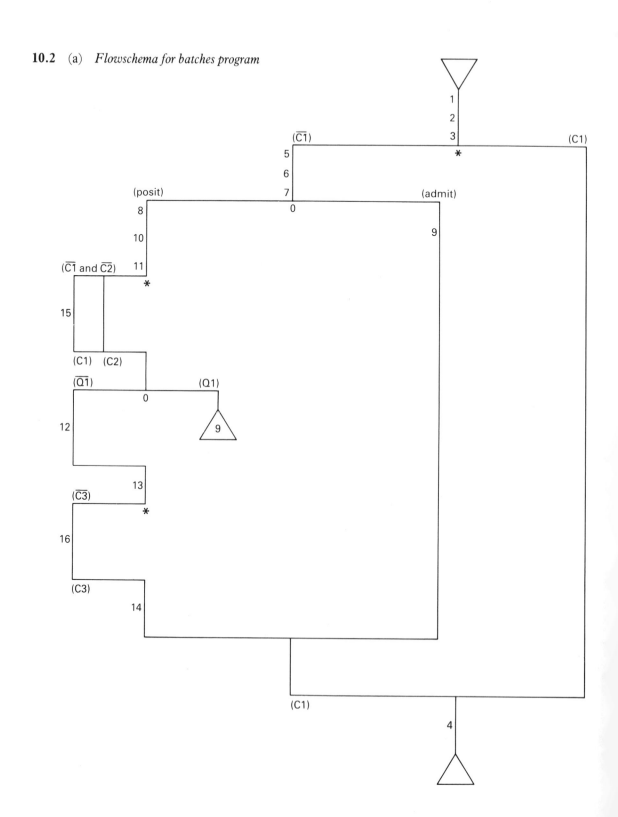

(b)   *Test paths for batches program*

Test path no.	Path conditions
1	$\overline{C1}$, $\overline{C1}$ and $\overline{C2}$, C1, $\overline{Q1}$, C3, (C3), (C1)
2	$\overline{C1}$, $\overline{C1}$ and $\overline{C2}$, C1, Q1, (C1)
3	$\overline{C1}$, $\overline{C1}$ and $\overline{C2}$, C2, $\overline{Q1}$, $\overline{C3}$, (C3), (C1)
4	$\overline{C1}$, $\overline{C1}$ and $\overline{C2}$, C2, Q1, (C1)
5	C1

11.1 *Project team members with job title module*
       database navigation structure

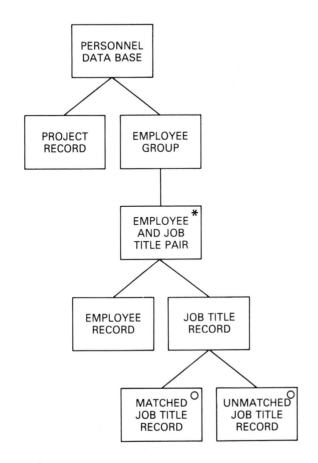

11.2   *Courses attended by department's employees module database navigation structure*

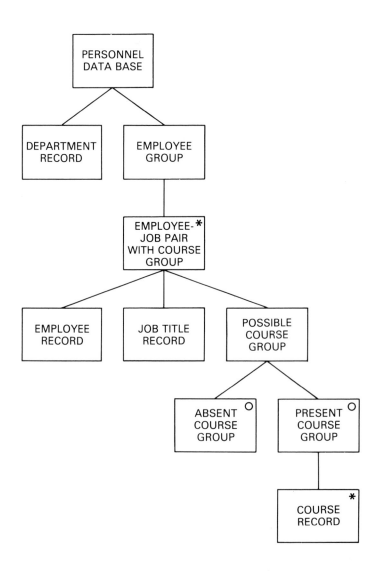

11.3   *Courses still to be attended module*
   (a)   *Database navigation structure*

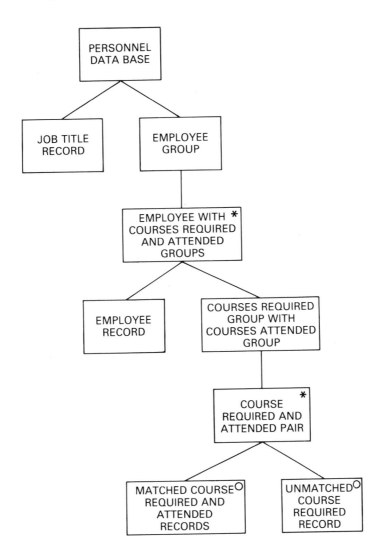

(b)   *Final program structure*

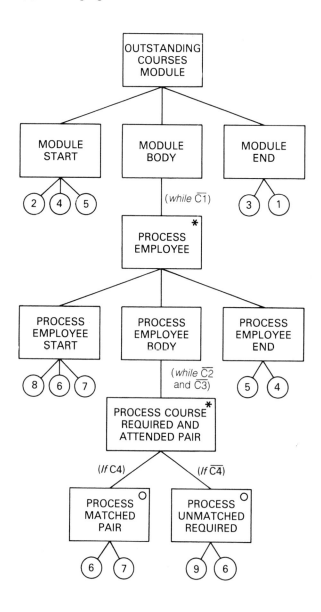

Conditions list
C1   end of employees-with-same-job set?
C2   end of courses-attended set?
C3   end of courses-required set?
C4   required-course-code =
     attended-course-code?

Actions list
1   exit module
2   ready data base
3   finish data base
4   find job-title record using job-id
5   obtain next employee record
    within employees-with-same-job set
6   obtain next course record within
    courses-required set
7   obtain next course record within
    courses-attended set
8   print employee-name
9   print course-name from
    course (required) record

12.1 (a) Optimization of selected components associated with component 5.
Reorder selected components as follows:

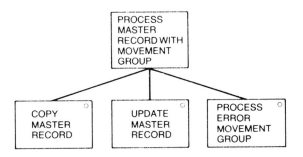

(b) Hive off components 7 and 10 as common subroutine.
(c) Action 11 in components 15 and 16 is a common action tail. Could change design in the area of component 13 as follows:

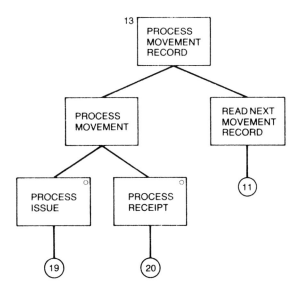

Index